*Experiences of God*

Jürgen Moltmann

---

# *Experiences of God*

**FORTRESS PRESS**        Philadelphia

Translated by Margaret Kohl from the German 'Der Gott, auf den ich hoffe', in *Warum ich Christ bin,* ed. Walter Jens, Kindler Verlag GmbH, Munich 1979, pp. 264–80 and *Gotteserfahrungen: Hoffnung, Angst, Mystik,* Christian Kaiser Verlag, Munich 1979.

First American Edition by Fortress Press 1980
Third printing 1984

---

**Library of Congress Cataloging in Publication Data**

Moltmann, Jürgen.
  Experiences of God.
  Translation of Der Gott auf den ich hoffe, from the anthology Warum ich Christ bin, and of Gotteserfahrungen, Hoffnung, Angst, Mystik.
    1. Hope—Collected works. 2. Anxiety—Collected works. 3. Mysticism—Collected works. 4. Moltmann, Jürgen—Collected works. I. Moltmann, Jürgen. Gotteserfahrungen. English. 1980. II. Title.
BV4638.M55513    230    80-8046
ISBN 0-8006-1406-2

---

1635L84   Printed in the United States of America   1-1406

# Contents

# Why am I a Christian?

What a curious question!

Who is interrogating me like this? Do I have to put my name to my answer? The question sounds inquisitive. Somebody wants to know the reasons that led somebody else to a particular conviction. It sounds impertinent too – as if the other person is bound to justify his decision to believe. The question can lead both the questioner and the person questioned astray; for does Christian existence really belong to the level of reasons and counter-reasons, for and against? Do the reasons produce the conviction, or does the conviction produce the reasons? Kierkegaard thought about this and decided that in questions of faith conviction creates the reasons, because the fundamental vital interest precedes all the arguments. On another level, Rilke was right too:

> Look at the lovers –
> how quickly they lie
> when the proofs begin!

Reasons can be used to bolster up something that is insecure in itself. Our own subjectivity can reveal itself in our arguments. But we can hide our subjectivity behind arguments too. Too many reasons are simply the expression of protestations and assurances which make the person unconvincing.

And yet the question 'why' has its own justification. To answer it is part of the reasonableness of faith. Why? Because faith – Christian faith at least – is not merely a matter of subjective feeling and vague beliefs. It is the definite perception and recognition of a history – the open history of Christ. Reason asks faith about the meaning of this history, and faith asks reason whether the history is really true. Faith is sure when it is serious and when it makes us free, when it is the faith of the heart, when it is a matter of personal experience and not a mild affair of custom. It is independent decision, not adaptation to the religion of a particular society. But just because it is the individual's most personal and most private affair, it is completely and wholly devotion to something bigger than ourselves, and something entirely different from ourselves. One of the earliest confessions of Christian faith, in the gospel of John, already brings this out: Peter says, 'We *have believed and have come to know* that you are the Holy One of God' (6.69).

What I accept in faith as being certainly true for myself, I accept perceptively in its own truth. What applies to me in faith, exists quite apart from me in what I perceive. In faith I relate God to myself. In what I perceive I relate myself to God. So in the interplay between faith and perception, truth is assured and assurance is true. This means that the question why I am a Christian requires an answer that is subjective and objective at the same time. The reasons must be comprehensible, communicable and acceptable, and the person who gives his reasons must, as his own self, with the history of his own life and his own irreplaceable subjectivity, be recognizable as the believer who is giving an account of his faith.

Consequently we cannot stand still at the question 'Why?'. The question 'Why?' has to be supplemented by the question 'Through what?' and 'How?'. Even if we ask inquisitively or impertinently why someone is a Christian, what we really

2

want to know too – and what we really have to know – is
how he became one, and through what. The arguments have
to be spread out on the table; but the story has to be told at
the table too. If reasons and conviction are so inextricably
linked in matters of faith, then the objective arguments
belong to the subjective history; for that is their context. But
the personal history of faith, for its part, is the story of how
someone has come to terms with these arguments.

If we wanted to lay all our stress on the arguments, and
concern ourselves only with reasons and counter-reasons, we
could easily lose sight altogether of the history of Christ, to
which Christian faith owes its existence, and of our own
personal history with this faith. The scholastic, orthodox
period of Christian theology shows this clearly enough.

If we wanted to lay all our stress on the history, then we
could only tell a story: re-tell the stories in the Bible, go on
to tell our personal story – and then put together a history
made up of a whole number of different narratives. The eras
of Christian mysticism and pietism make this plain. But don't
the two things belong indissolubly together – the arguments
of reason and the stories that make up the history?

If the arguments of reason express what is universal and
necessary, the stories that make up the history bring out
what is individual and contingent. Christianity, like Judaism,
is a historical faith, for it springs from a history which faith
remembers and makes a matter of present experience in its
own testimony. This is the history of Christ. We testify to it
through the experience of our own history with this history
of Christ. But as faith, Christian faith points to the present
existence of a future that does not pass away historically like
everything else, which comes but does not remain. As faith
in God it goes beyond history, thrusting forward to that
endless liberty from guilt and death which hope apprehends
and defines in the symbols of the kingdom of God, the
resurrection of the dead and 'the new creation'. In order to

3

communicate the particular remembrance of the history of
Christ and the restless hope for the kingdom of freedom
which continually pushes forward, we shall have to learn to
tell as we argue and to argue as we tell.

This becomes particularly clear when we come to the greatest scruple which this 'curious question' evokes in the person
who is to sign his name to the answer. Why am I a Christian?
Well, *am* I really a Christian? Am I so firmly and definitely
a Christian that I can produce arguments to support the fact,
as if it were something finished and done with, and open to
proof? What is the position if this 'being' of mine continually
slips away from me when I want to lay hold of it as firmly
as the question suggests? What if this 'being a Christian'
which I am being asked about is not something that *is* at all?
What if it is something that is involved in a continual process
of *becoming*? What if our self-examination has to confess:
I am a Christian and a non-Christian at the same time? Faith
and doubt struggle within me, so that I have continually to
cry out: 'Lord I believe; help my unbelief!' What if I am
again and again thrown back to the beginning, where being
and non-being wrestle with one another? For then I cannot
produce any arguments for a complete and secure Christian
existence. Then I have after all simply to *tell* about these
threshold conflicts. This story of conflict can certainly provide other people with reasons for beginning to become a
Christian; but the completion of this 'becoming' into 'being'
is still ahead, both for the narrator and the listener.

It is the old experience so often shared by believers: '*Chris-
tianus semper est in fieri*', says Luther. A Christian's *being*
is in *becoming*. His becoming is a continual repentance, a
continual new start in a new direction. It is a new start from
sin to righteousness, from slavery to freedom, from doubt to
faith, and from past to future. That is why the Christian's
being is still hidden in the womb of the divine future. 'It does
not yet appear what we shall be' (I John 3.2). Anyone who

4

starts off all too rashly from the assumption that he is a Christian and therefore only has to be responsible for the 'why', loses the liberty of his own future, because he has forgotten that his own being is still hidden in its becoming. Because it is still hidden, and because being a Christian has a future quality about it, it is usually easier to say what a Christian is not, rather than what he is. In this passing and transitory world the true Christian is a man without a name, an extraneous element, a mysterious exception, a lonely harbinger of God's future.

And yet in the midst of the restless struggle for faith and the continually new 'beginning to be a Christian', there is a curiously peaceful assurance about one's own being, a profound trust which is the only thing that makes sense of the whole struggle, with all its contradictions and vexations. I cannot argue myself into it. Nor can I achieve it by moral effort and religious conflicts of conscience. But it is manifested to me out of the history of Christ, and I find a continual witness to it in people and events round about me. To put it simply: God is for me; I am his child. Christ is beside me; I am his brother. Whether this makes me believe more strongly or whether I doubt all the more, whether I am swallowed up in the darkness of night or find myself at the dawn of a new day — I know: there is someone waiting for me, who will not give me up, who goes ahead of me, who lifts me up, someone to whom I am important.

In the New Testament this spark of certainty in the uncertainty of the struggle, this element of being in the ups and downs of becoming, is called being God's child. The favourite and much quoted text, 'It does *not yet appear* what we shall be' is therefore preceded by a declaration of confidence: 'Beloved, we are God's children *now*.' It is this trust, after all, which spurs hope on; and it this very *being* of God's children which is in the process of *becoming* in the Christian's life and death.

If I gather together the Christian's believing and perceiving, his arguing and telling, his being and becoming, then I can really only answer that 'curious question' with a short theological biography. Why I am a Christian and how I came to be one; what signposts and experiences led me along the way of theological perception in particular (since this has come to be my life) – all this has to be described if I am to do justice to the question. Enough will remain unanswered in any case.

## II  THE GOD IN WHOM I HOPE

Born in Hamburg in 1926, I belong to the generation which consciously lived through the horrors of the Second World War, the collapse of an empire and all its institutions, the guilt and shame of one's own nation, and a long period as prisoner of war. Later we were called 'the sceptical generation'. And those of us who survived those years and who came back from the camps and hospitals were certainly burnt children who from then on shunned the fire. We had learnt justifiable mistrust. But we were really neither sceptical nor resigned. We were weighed down by the sombre burden of a guilt which could never be paid off; and what we felt about life was an inconsolable grief. It is understandable that there were some of us whose motto was 'count me out', and whose aim was to withdraw into private life for the future. But really we came back to Germany with the will to create a new, different, more humane world. Some of us found behind the barbed wire the power of a hope which wants something new, instead of seeking a return to the old.

Our Abitur – the university extrance exam – was put forward so that we could be sent to the guns, as Air Force auxiliaries. At that time I really wanted to read mathematics and physics at the university. Of course I had become interested in these subjects at school because of some teachers I

6

admired. The theory of relativity and quantum physics were the most fascinating secrets open to knowledge. At that time the idea of theology was as remote as the church itself. The 'iron rations' in the way of reading matter which I took with me into the miseries of war were Goethe's poems and the works of Nietzsche (army edition, India paper). In February 1945 I was taken prisoner by the British, and for over three years I was moved about from camp to camp in Belgium, Scotland and England. In April 1948 I was one of the last to be 'repatriated', as the phrase went.

The break-up of the German front, the collapse of law and humanity, the self-destruction of German civilization and culture, and finally the appalling end on 9 May 1945 – all this was followed by the revelation of the crimes which had been committed in Germany's name – Buchenwald, Auschwitz, Maidanek, Bergen-Belsen and the rest. And with that came the necessity of standing up to it all inwardly, shut up in camps as we were. I think my own little world fell to pieces then too. The 'iron rations' I had with me were quickly used up, and what remained left a stale taste in the mouth. In that Belgian camp, hungry as we were, I saw how other men collapsed inwardly, how they gave up all hope, sickening for the lack of it, some of them dying. The same thing almost happened to me. What kept me from it was a rebirth to new life thanks to a hope for which there was no evidence at all.

It was not that I experienced any sudden conversion. What I felt all at once was the death of all the mainstays that had sustained my life up to then. It was only slowly that something different began to build up in their stead. At home, Christianity was only a matter of form. One came across it once a year at Christmas time, as something rather remote. In the prison camps where I was I only met it in very human – all too human – form. It was nothing very overwhelming. And yet the experience of misery and forsakenness and daily humiliation gradually built up into an experience of God.

It was the experience of God's presence in the dark night of the soul: 'If I make my bed in hell, behold, thou art there.' A well-meaning army chaplain had given me a New Testament. I thought it was out of place. I would rather have had something to eat. But then I became fascinated by the Psalms (which were printed in an appendix) and especially by Psalm 39: 'I was dumb with silence, I held my peace, even from good; and my sorrow was stirred' (but the German is much stronger – 'I have to eat up my grief within myself') . . . Hold thou not thy peace at my tears: for I am a stranger with thee, and a sojourner, as all my fathers were.' These psalms gave me the words for my own suffering. They opened my eyes to the God who is with those 'that are of a broken heart'. He was present even behind the barbed wire – no, most of all behind the barbed wire. But whenever in my despair I wanted to lay firm hold on this experience, it eluded me again, and there I was with empty hands once more. All that was left was an inward drive, a longing which provided the impetus to hope. How often I walked round and round in circles at night in front of the barbed wire fence. My first thoughts were always about the free world outside, from which I was cut off; but I always ended up thinking about a centre to the circle in the middle of the camp – a little hill, with a hut on it which served as a chapel. It seemed to me like a circle surrounding the mystery of God, which was drawing me towards it.

This experience of not sinking into the abyss but of being held up from afar was the beginning of a clear hope, without which it is impossible to live at all. At the same time, even this hope cut two ways; on the one hand it provided the strength to get up again after every inward or outward defeat; on the other hand it made the soul rub itself raw on the barbed wire, making it impossible to settle down in captivity or come to terms with it.

God in the dark night of the soul – God as the power of

hope and pain: this was the experience which moulded me in what are a person's most receptive years, between 18 and 21. I am reluctant to say that this is why I became a Christian, because that sounds like joining a party. Because I believe that I owe my survival to these experiences, I cannot even say I found God there. But I do know in my heart that it is there that he found me, and that I would otherwise have been lost.

Perhaps there are certain deeply rooted experiences in every life which mould existence and sustain it at the same time. We return to them again and again, recalling them and thinking them over. We continually give them a new interpretation. As we enter into them they become present, and the time that cuts us off from them ceases to exist. We experience ourselves as being still the same person, though new and different things have been added. We find our identity of being in all the changes life brings. That is the way I still experience today what I went through over thirty years ago. It was those experiences that induced me to give up my dream of mathematics and physics, Einstein and Planck, and study theology. This made me the first 'black sheep' in my 'enlightened' Hamburg family. But I found theology – *cum ira et studio* – a fascinating adventure, though a dangerous one too. One gets involved both in the material itself and personally, and one can only stand up to it by exerting all one's heart and all one's soul and all one's strength.

### III

When we were released from the prisoner of war camp in 1948 I felt like Jacob after his nocturnal struggle with the angel – with a lame hip, but crying, 'I will not let thee go except thou bless me.' The feeling was certainly somewhat exaggerated. And if at all, the blessing only consisted in being posted to another field of battle – West Germany in 1948.

In 1948 restoration had already set in, instead of the new beginning. Under the leadership of the inflexible and ruthlessly unfeeling Adenauer, there was reconstruction 'without experiments'. Under the leadership of the inflexible and quite unteachable Bishop Dibelius, the Protestant *Landeskirchen* – the regionally autonomous churches – were restored in their pre-1933 form. Even the much admired leaders of the 'Confessing church' did not build up any new church from below, out of the confessing congregations, which had been organized on a brotherly and advisory basis during the period of resistance. Instead they took possession of the traditional offices in the *Landeskirchen* and poured their new wine into the old bottles. Was the 'zero-point chance' missed? Or did the zero point perhaps not possess the potentiality we ascribed to it? In those years, when the old conditions were being so obstinately restored, I myself and people like me grew increasingly uneasy over this 'utopia of the *status quo*'. For it is pure utopia simply to want to preserve what one has, without risking anything new and better. And this 'utopia of the *status quo*' seemed to us the worst of all utopias. I took part in a series of protests at that time: against the rearmament of the Federal Republic; against the atom bomb; against the church's willingness to supply chaplains to the armed forces; and other things. I worked in a German-Polish society for reconciliation with Poland. But these actions were not particularly effective at the time. The great breakthrough, mentally and politically, only came in the 60s.

After I had taken my degree in 1952 I took up practical congregational work and became pastor in Bremen-Wasserhorst. In 1957 I finished my professorial thesis in Göttingen, and in 1958 was appointed to a chair at the Kirchliche Hochschule in Wuppertal, which had been founded by the Confessing church. After five years of practical work, theology was now my main job again, although at the same time I had not the faintest idea how one could go on teaching theology on one's own after Karl Barth's monumental *Church Dogmatics.* Surely he had already said everything there was to say, and said it once and for all? It was only in 1957 that the Dutch theologian Arnold von Ruler had begun to free me from this error. Through him I came to know the theology of the apostolate, and the fallow ground of eschatology, and the courage to deal imaginatively with dogmatics, though my own visions were moving in another direction at that time. And then I came across Ernst Bloch (at that time still teaching in Leipzig). *Das Prinzip Hoffnung* – 'the principle of hope' – was an epoch-making experience. I read it while I was on holiday in Ticino, and the beauty of the Swiss mountains passed me by unnoticed. My first and lasting impression was: why has Christian theology paid no attention to the subject of hope? Surely this is a theme it ought to make its very own? Where is the early Christian spirit of hope in Christianity today? I began to work on the *Theology of Hope,* which came out in 1964 (in English in 1967); and now suddenly all the different threads of biblical theology, the theology of the apostolate, hope for the kingdom of God and the philosophy of hope all came together, like a pattern for a tapestry, where everything matched. I had no intention of playing heir to Ernst Bloch, nor did I become one of his followers. What I was thinking of was a parallel theological treatment of the philosophy of hope on the basis of the Christian faith's own presuppositions and perspectives.

Christianity is completely and entirely and utterly hope – a looking forward and a forward direction; hope is not just an appendix. So Christianity inevitably means a new setting forth and a transformation of the present. Eschatology (the doctrine of the Last Things) is not just one of Christianity's many doctrines. It is quite simply the medium of the Christian faith, the keynote, the daybreak colours of a new expected day which bathe everything in their light. For the Christian faith lives from the raising of the crucified Christ and reaches out towards the promises of Christ's universal future. But that means that the hoping person can never come to terms with the laws and necessities of this world. He can never come to terms with the inescapability of death or with the evil that continually breeds evil. For him the resurrection of Christ is not merely consolation in suffering; it is also the sign of God's protest against suffering. That is why whenever faith develops into hope it does not make people serene and placid; it makes them restless. It does not make them patient; it makes them impatient. Instead of being reconciled to existing reality they begin to suffer from it and to resist it.

For me, these perceptions meant a great liberation at that time. They swept me out of my apathy and my vague disquiet over the intellectual and political situation, and the situation in the churches. They presented me with a guiding passion. The resonance which the *Theology of Hope* found from 1964 onwards in West and East, and in the Third World, shows that this subject was 'in the air'. To be allowed to hope again means being reborn. This is true not merely personally, but socially and politically too.

The 60s were brimming over with movements of hope and experiences of rebirth and renewal; and particularly at the very places where the springs had seemed to have dried up completely. The *Aggiornamento* ran through the Roman Catholic church. Vatican II was opened in the spirit of John XXIII. Reforms which no outsider would have thought possible became reality. Within a few years anti-Protestant controversial theology disappeared, giving way to a new ecumenical theology. A humanist wave ran through European Marxism as its self-destruction through Stalinism was surmounted. Socialism began to flower again, as if an ice-age had ended. Our Christian-Marxist dialogues began to get moving. And whereas only a few years before, the Marxist – in complete possession of the one and only truth – gave answers to questions which no one had asked, we now suddenly met with a new Marxist generation which was able to enquire, which no longer annihilated its partner as an ideological opponent, but was prepared to recognize him for what he was. The Christian-Marxist encounter, as we set out together from our different camps and fronts, was one of the happiest intellectual experiences of those years. Even though that dialogue was forcibly destroyed later, it is a phenomenon which cannot be forgotten – a sign of hope for better times.

These new, hopeful beginnings reached their peak in 1968. In Prague, we saw with Alexander Dubcek 'socialism with a human face'. For a moment of world history it meant hope for Western and Eastern Europe. In Rome, Vatican II came to an end. In Medellin the Latin American episcopal conference gave the signal for the church's renewal out of 'grass-roots' congregations, and for the liberation of the people. In Uppsala the fourth General Assembly of the World Council of Churches took as its motto the greatest promise of the Christian hope: 'Behold I make all things new.' In 1968 the civil rights movement reached its peak in the United States. In Paris we saw the May student revolts. In West Germany a peace policy towards other states and a policy of internal reform was finally firmly initiated.

But 1968 also already heralded the reaction and the breakdown of hope. The march into Czechoslovakia by Warsaw pact troops robbed socialism of its 'human face'. The murders of John F. Kennedy and Martin Luther King, and the crass absurdity of the Vietnam war, spread fear and anger. The student protest movement was misinterpreted. Brutality developed on both sides. And a conservative 'Evangelical' movement was formed, in opposition to the ecumenical activism that had followed Uppsala.

Experiences like this are experiences of hope: the experiences of a new setting forth out of stagnation, and the experiences of contradiction and disappointment. In the 60s we

13

saw a great many different hopes, which collapsed in resignation or anger or violence under the pressure of the first
opposition. Genuine hope is not blind optimism. It is hope
with open eyes, which sees the suffering and yet believes in
the future. It is only out of disappointment that hope can
become wise.

## IV

At the end of the 60s Johann-Baptist Metz and I tried to
develop a political theology out of 'the theology of hope', so
as to arrive at *hope in action* out of the hope of faith. I also
tried to break down the moral compulsion to action, which
is inherent in activism, through the discovery of *life as a
feast*, and theology's aesthetic categories. But in the face of
growing difficulties and disappointments in the movements
I have mentioned, in which I had been passionately involved,
the other fundamental experience came to the fore again,
personally and theologically: the experience of God in the
experience of forsakenness and desolation. I took this up in
the form of a 'theology of the cross', which was published
in 1972 under the title of *Der gekreuzigte Gott* (*The Crucified God* appeared two years later).

At that time there was plenty of criticism of the church
and the Christian faith from outside. Sociological and
psychological analyses threatened to rob Christianity of its
Christian identity, and to expose it as the religious phenomenon accompanying late capitalist society. Christianity
itself had provided reason enough for this. Consequently
many people asked what was special or individual about
Christianity – what was specifically Christian?

What is special about Christianity is the thing that makes
it a stumbling-block, because it simply cannot be got rid of:
the cross of Christ on Golgotha. It is this crucified Christ
who stands at the centre of faith, the church and Christianity.

What is really Christian can be discovered in the light of the cross. At the same time the crucified Jesus is himself the most stringent criticism of Christian superstition, Christian illusion and Christian timidity. The only idea of God – the only vision of hope – the only act that can be called Christian is the one that can endure before the face of the dying, forsaken Christ. But what theology *can* endure in the face of Jesus' dying cry, 'My God, why has thou forsaken me'? Either, as I wrote then, the crucified Jesus is the end of all theology and 'God is dead', or he is the beginning of the theology that deserves the name of Christian. What hope can endure beneath the cross? Surely only a hope which springs from the death of the person who is stamped by his old, personal, dominating interests. What act can endure? Surely only the act that frees men and women from the powers of evil and suffering. If the cross breaches the unquestioned continuities of life and thought, then a theology which wants to lead us to liberty with hope must continually come back to this breach. It is only the naked harshness of the cross on Golgotha that is capable from saving us from the harshness of life and death.

For me, the work on this theology of the cross meant a surprising turning-point. Having asked in many different ways what the cross of Christ means for the church, for theology, for discipleship, for culture and society, I now found myself faced with the reverse question: what does Christ's cross really mean for God himself? Is God so absolute and sovereign that he reigns in heavenly glory, incapable of suffering and untouched by the death of his Son? And if God is essentially incapable of suffering, does this not mean that he is incapable of love as well? But if he is incapable of love, he is poorer than any man or woman who is able to love and suffer.

The more I am bound to take the presence of God in Jesus' suffering and death seriously, the more deeply I must ask that other question, about the presence of Jesus' suffering and death in God. A God who is eternally only in love with himself, and therefore without any concern for others, is a monster, an idol. Like many other theologians, I found the way to the mystery of God's inner passion opening up from the cross of Christ: 'God is love.' And from the cross of Christ I also found access to the trinitarian life of God. I have called this the trinitarian theology of the cross. Here the doctrine of the Trinity is no longer a theological speculation, and the crucified Jesus is no longer merely an object of Christian piety. On the cross of Christ God cuts himself off from himself. He delivers himself up in order to be ours and to be with us, right into the desolation of God-forsakenness itself. Even in this hell, thou art there. That is the divine truth of Jesus' cry of desolation. And that is why, on the other hand, we cannot shut out any suffering or any loss or any grief from God. If we discover God in forsakenness and desolation, and if every forsakenness we have to endure is taken up in God, then we even win back the elements of truth in pantheism. 'In him we live and move and have our being.' Nothing is shut off from God, if God himself has gone through the experience of Christ's cross. Without the cross pantheism is an illusion, which falls to pieces when a single child dies. But with the cross of Christ as its foundation, pantheism shows God's immensity and breadth.

The doctrine of the Trinity really always counted as being a product of Hellenistically influenced, philosophical theology. Adolf von Harnack wanted to eliminate it altogether for that reason, in order to get back to the simple gospel of Jesus, God the Father, and the immortality of the soul. That was before the First World War. Today we have been surprised to discover Israelite and Jewish contours in the history of the passion and the doctrine of the Trinity. As early as 1936 Rabbi Abraham Heschel rejected the axiom that God was incapable of suffering, and developed a doctrine of God's 'pathos', his suffering, out of the theology of the Old Testament prophets. Even earlier Franz Rosenzweig had interpreted the mystical doctrine of the Shekina, the indwelling of God, in this way:

God himself cuts himself off from himself, he gives himself away to his people, he suffers with their sufferings, he goes with them into the misery of the foreign land, he wanders with their wanderings.[1]

This knowledge of the God who suffers with his people and wanders with his people's wanderings kept alive the hope of the Jewish people in suffering and the experience of death. If God himself suffers with us in our persecutions and pain, then we can resist adaptation and self-destruction. This message, it seems to me, is also the message of the God who humiliated himself in Christ. 'Only the suffering God can help us', wrote Dietrich Bonhoeffer from his prison cell.[2]

## V

Why am I a Christian? In order to answer this question I have had to put it to myself, and have told something of my own life and my own growth in perception. The personal elements in this account cannot be transferred to anyone else, any more than my own 'self' – the self who was asked the question – can be transferred to anyone else. Have I given reason enough why I am a Christian, or why I am becoming one? Who can judge? Who sets the standard? What may be enough for me may be totally insufficient for someone else. What may be an overwhelming experience for someone else may leave me cold. So, in the end, let me stand aside from all the arguments and all the telling. Let me say what I have to say very simply:

I am a Christian for Christ's sake.

I found my desolation in him, and found God in my

desolation. In him I found the power of a hope which I can believe, live and die with. But whether this means that I am a Christian – that I really do not know, in spite of all the arguments and in spite of all the telling. Neither I nor anyone else can decide. It is in the hands of the one to whom I trust myself.

# Hope

## 1 The Command to Hope

Men and women are called to enduring hope. True hope is not based on the ebb and flow of our feelings. Nor does it come from success in life. True hope — which means the hope that endures and sustains us — is based on God's call and command. We are called to hope. It is a command: a command to resist death. It is a call: the call to divine life.

Enduring hope is not something innate, something we possess from birth. Nor do we acquire it from experience. We have to learn it. We learn to hope if we obey the call. We learn to hope in the experiences life brings us. We come to know its truth if we are forced to stand our ground against despair. We come to know its power when we realize that it keeps us alive in the midst of death.

Is there really something like a *call* to hope? Can we actually be *commanded* to hope? Is hope a *duty*?

To maintain any of these things will sound unusual to anyone who thinks that hope is an impulse of the heart, or mere youthful exuberance. It will sound strange too to all the people who have based their hope on experience, or on being able to calculate what is going to happen in history. What I myself have learnt from my own experience of hope is this. Hope is more than feeling. Hope is more than experience. Hope is more than foresight. Hope is a command. Obeying it means life, survival, endurance, standing up to life until death is swallowed up in victory. Obeying it means never giving way to the forces of annihilation in resignation or rage. 'It is not so much our sins that bring disaster upon us; it is despair', said Chrysostom, one of the Fathers of the church. Today we call this frustration. The command to hope, on the other hand, is the power behind all the commandments which preserve life and show us the way to liberty. It says, 'Because I live you will live also.' It says, 'He who endures to the end will be saved.'

What does the command to hope require of us today? What gives us the power to hope?

First of all, let me discuss our loss of hope and show where our hope has been buried, describing the situations where hope turned into fear of the future. After that I should like to talk about the faith which makes a new beginning possible, and about the practice of the hope which can be re-won. Thirdly, I should like to show that our hope has been given back to us, retrieved and born again through the future of Jesus Christ; and I will try to explain *how* this comes about through Christ's future.

## 2 *The Things that Contradict Hope*

'Called to hope' is a biblical phrase. It is an expression of the whole life of the New Testament's community of hope. The person who believes knows that he has been born again to a living hope. Through Christ's resurrection from the dead an incomparable future has been thrown open to hope – incomparable because it is imperishable. Indestructible and sure, the kingdom of God's liberty and peace stands open, for the renewal of heaven and earth. The person who believes is prepared to 'account for the hope that is in him' to everyone: to the judge who can throw him into prison as well as to the infuriated masses. The new people of God is born out of the hope of Christ – born of Jews and Gentiles, masters and slaves, men and women, humanity and creation. The Bible, both the Old and New Testaments, is in sober fact the book of God's promises and man's hopes.

'Called to hope' – this was the motto of the General Assembly of the Evangelical churches in Germany in 1979. It is by no means an expression of what respectable middle-class Christianity and the organized religion of West Germany feels about life. On the contrary, what we really feel is anxiety: that vague, oppressive feeling about what is going to happen which always expects the worst, and the gloom which does not believe oneself or other people capable of anything positive. Anxiety is the reason why so many people only see the future as a threat to the present; they no longer view it as a chance for something new. Anxiety is the reason why many young people are not just afraid of death, but are already afraid of life. Anxiety is the reason why many people no longer understand what is going on in the world and look round for scapegoats among its leaders. The general anxiety is laying us open to public blackmail, and so it is making us aggressive and angry. The most that many people hope for from the future is that they will go on possessing what they have at present, and that the annual rate of growth will be secured. And it is just this, moreover, that they were promised in New Year speeches and addresses. Let us not complain about that here. But we have to ask, quite specifically: *when* did we destroy our future? *Where* did we bury our hopes? Let me quite frankly mention three things through which, as I believe, we have destroyed our future, so that our hope has been transformed into fear.

(*a*) There is only one people of hope in the world. It is the one people of God, the people of the old *and* the new covenant. Because Jews and Christians have a common hope for

21

'the one who is to come', the Messiah, they are on the way together to God's kingdom and future. That is why they are persecuted together and suffer together. When Israel is led to the slaughter the church goes with her – if things are as they should be. But when this happened in the holocaust of the Third Reich the churches in Germany were not of the party. They signed agreements, fought for their own survival, and saved – themselves. Certainly, a few individuals went with the Jews and were faithful to their common hope. Certainly, a few individuals threw open their homes to the persecuted, were persecuted themselves and kept love alive in the midst of public hate. These few individuals are the upholders of hope down to the present day. But the churches as a whole were too much state churches, and trusted too much to 'the powers that be' for them to seek their hope together with Israel. Christians betrayed their own future and buried their own hopes in Auschwitz and Maidanek and in the other death camps. They buried them by their silence and by turning away from the Jews. Where the Jewish people of hope were annihilated, the Christian hope was annihilated too. It seems to me that we must be quite clear about this: our hope turned into anxiety as a result of our silence over the annihilation of the Jewish hope. It has turned into the anxiety of guilt. The key to the rebirth of our hope is to be found in Auschwitz.

(*b*) Widespread discouragement is growing everywhere in the affluent societies. What has anxiety to do with affluence and prosperity? In theory nothing at all. But in actual fact a great deal. Anxiety is connected with prosperity based on injustice, with prosperity at the cost of other people and other nations. Are we in the West living at the cost of the poorer nations? The spokesmen of those nations say we are. Your hope, they say, is our despair. The spokesmen of our industry and politics deny it. But our fear of the future knows better. It is impossible to be happy, and impossible to be hopeful, if one is sitting on an island of prosperity in the midst of a continually rising sea of poverty. One can only defend oneself against this sea of hungry people by simply ceasing to look at them, by raising the customs barriers against their products, by selling industrial goods at too high a price and by paying back alms out of the profits in the form of development aid – though not even 0.7% of our own gross national product in West Germany. But then there ceases to be any future for us to *hope* for. By securing what they possess against the claims of the poor nations, the rich ones are destroying their own future and burying their own hope. A growing sense of helplessness and perplexity and general gloom, even cynicism, about these questions is symptomatic. The key to the rebirth of our hope lies in the place where we buried it: in the exploited and oppressed nations and their liberation.

(c) Finally, the hopes which our societies invested in the building up of industrial power have long since come up against 'the limits of growth'. Pollution, the destruction of nature and the perilous risks of nuclear power plants are all pointing to the end of a road. It is true that our superstitious faith in rates of growth is still so unbroken that we are prepared to make sacrifices for it. But this superstition is slowly but surely turning into anguish. The spiritual crises which are spreading everywhere correspond to the economic ones, because many people feel that although we can build ourselves palaces, we are digging the grave for creation and our own selves at the same time. This is not the way to fulfil what we hope for; it is the way to bury hope. We shall not win any future *against* the natural world we live in. If nature is irrevocably destroyed, our future will be at an end. The key to the rebirth of our hope is to be found in the place where we are threatening to destroy the future of creation.

As long as our future drives other people to despair,
as long as our prosperity means poverty for others,
as long as our 'growth' destroys nature –
anxiety, not hope, will be our daily companion.


### 3 Faith which makes a New Beginning Possible

Faith which throws open the future is first of all a faith
which makes a new beginning possible. The new beginning
is the practice of living hope. The person who has no hope,
the person who sees no hope ahead, cannot make a fresh
start. People used sometimes to call this new beginning
'repentance'. But in German the word that means repentance
can also mean 'penance', 'expiation' – a kind of punishment.
The person does penance; he goes on punishing himself until
he has worked off whatever he has done wrong in the past.
In the Bible, however, repentance means 'con-version', an
'about turn'. And this turn is *a turn to the future*. It is a turn
to the future of the living God, and therefore a turning away
from death and all the powers that destroy life. Hope for the
future is only possible if the past is honestly recognized and
accepted, without any self-justification Of course every turning away from something is painful, even a turning away
from the paths that lead to death. It is painful because we
have to say goodbye to old familiar habits. But joy in the
future of life is incomparably greater. That is why we are
told in Luke's gospel that *repentance means the joy of God
and man* (15.10ff.). The movement of repentance, the movement towards a new beginning, brings hope into our lives
again. It is only through repentance that we can once more
be certain of our future.

Repentance wants to lay hold on *the whole of life*. Though
repentance means 're-thinking', we do not make a new
beginning simply through a mere change of mind. Repentance means the *practice* of a new life. It is not achieved

merely through good intentions. Everything which is brought into the movement of repentance becomes full of hope. But everything that remains outside it remains dead and meaningless. That is why there is a fresh start towards the future politically and economically too. Anyone who stops short half-way in the movement of repentance, interpreting it as purely a matter of the heart – as merely religious or spiritual – is hindering his future and destroying his hope. Theological and ecclesiastical institutions must be clear about this as well: middle-class ideologies and religions which are a branch of the administration do not throw open the future or make a new beginning possible. They live from anxiety, and only disseminate a deceptive sense of security.

At what points is the faith which makes a new beginning possible relevant today?

Faith which makes a new beginning possible is relevant today, first, when Christians turn to the Jews, and the churches to Israel. 'To go on existing as a Jew after Auschwitz is a command of hope', wrote the Jewish philosopher Emil Fackenheim. To be both a Christian and a German after Auschwitz is above all else a command to remember, contrary to all the forgetfulness we may wish for. We can only find our hope again if we resolve never to forget. It is only then that there is a future for us after Auschwitz. Anyone who suppresses this past, or who fails to stand up to the burden of our past, gives Hitler a posthumous victory. The readiness for absolute and unqualified truth must go together with the renunciation of any kind of self-justification. This does not only apply to the individual. It applies even more to institutions – the church, for example. The hope which liberates us for a new future will become possible again to the degree in which we labour in grief to accept our past. Then we shall also find the happiness of discovering that – as Martin Buber aptly remarked – Christians and Jews have two things in common: a book and a hope. The fellowship of Jews and Christians in this hope today also includes mutual participation in their separate histories – and this means the history of Israel as country and state as well.

Faith which makes a new beginning possible is relevant today, secondly, when we sit down at table with the poor and oppressed peoples, and share their burdens. Development aid and relief funds for feeding and supporting the hungry are necessary, because otherwise many people would starve. But this is only a temporary measure. Building up a just world-wide economic order has absolute priority. The question is not what we can give them, but when we are going to stop taking things away from them. The poor nations are not our 'problem'. It is we – the rich, industrial nations – who are *their* problem. And their problem is going to be either solved or accentuated here, among us or by us. At the end of the war in Germany there was a *Lastenausgleich*, an 'equalization of burdens', which meant that the people who had been driven out of the former German territories in the east were compensated for the property they had lost. The scheme itself was imperfect, but the idea was right. An equalization of burdens is not a question of 'aid'. It is a matter of justice. We must all bear the misery of hunger, child mortality and unemployment in the world *together*. We cannot solve the question by increasing our contributions to charity. The only answer to this mass misery is a new community and fellowship. Ecumenicity and solidarity begin with shared suffering. Riches that are witheld impoverish the poor and make the rich lonely and sad. We gain something too through an equal distribution of burdens. We regain the trust of other nations and we gain fellowship with other people. Is this fellowship not more valuable than the rates of growth of our own prosperity? There is only hope at a common table. The Messiah will only come when *all* his guests have sat down at table, says a hopeful old Jewish saying. Don't Christians believe that Jesus the Messiah has come *in order that* all his guests can sit down at the same table? Why are we stopping them?

Faith which makes a new beginning possible is relevant today, thirdly, in our community with the natural environment. Up to now man has chosen to find the way to freedom by way of exploitation – exploitation of natural resources and exploitation of human labour. This attitude was understandable enough in the era when men and women were at the mercy of natural forces which they did not understand. Exploitation turned man from a slave into the lord of creation. This road is coming to an end. It no longer leads to greater freedom. It is becoming a new dependency. For it was ultimately man himself who was the uncertain factor that had to be overcome before he could enter the atomic age. The risks of nuclear power and the electronic surveillance of the whole population are the beginning of the destruction of human health and human dignity. But before fear of themselves drives people to collective self-destruction, we ought to turn round and make a new beginning. Our hope lies in a new pact with nature. The old interpretation of nature was that, since it 'belonged to no one in particular', it could be thrown open to exploitation. This, as the prophet says, was a pact with death – the death of nature. The new pact will be a pact of co-operation, symbiosis and recognition that the natural world around us has a right to live. It is only a pact of this kind which will lead to life. It is only in this way that hope for the future will become possible again. This is the only road that leads to freedom, if true freedom means friendship, not lordship.

## 4   *The New Beginning that Finds the Future*

Anyone who is afraid of the future cannot make a new beginning even if he wants to. Anyone who believes that the world is going to end in catastrophe will not make a new beginning, because it is pointless. Anyone who sees no future before him goes on as before, until he falls backwards into the pit he is digging for himself. For a new beginning we need the power of a hope which transforms life and overcomes the world. But we only discover the power of a hope like this when we find the foundation for hope and recognize it clearly. By the foundation for hope I do not mean well-weighed arguments in favour of hope. I mean the living sources from which this power springs. The living source of hope lies in a future from which new time, new potentiality and new freedom continually advance to meet us. We find this future in Jesus Christ; he is our future – he is our hope. In the new beginning which faith makes possible we find Christ, who is our future and our hope. What does this mean? I should like to define it more precisely by taking three points of reference.

*(a) Born anew to a living hope through the resurrection of Jesus Christ from the dead*

Christ's resurrection and our rebirth belong together (I Peter 1.3). The one does not exist without the other. The beginning of the new life of hope in ourselves is our answer to this great new turn of events – of all events – which we call Christ's resurrection from the dead. At the same time his resurrection from the dead aims at our rebirth from anxiety into hope, so that our rebirth may lead to the rebirth of everything else.

Anyone who has grasped what Easter means has found an enduring hope. That is true. Anyone who is filled with this enduring hope in the light of Easter cannot be indifferent to the short-term hopes of everyday life. On the contrary, our daily hope is kindled by our enduring hope, and enduring hope acts like a purifying fire on the hopes of everyday, burning away the germs of vanity and the canker of resignation, both judging and raising up.

But does this not mean taking the resurrection of Christ in a literal and physical sense? And for that do we not require historical proofs? Let me just say briefly here that I consider historical proofs for what is provable in history to be extremely useful. To prove something always means fitting something new into the system of what already exists. But our history is dominated by guilt, suffering and death. Christ's resurrection from the dead calls this very history and this whole system of guilt, suffering and death in question. Consequently the resurrection is not open to proof *within the limits of this system.* It used to be said that this world cannot endure the righteousness of God; so the divine righteousness that is to come will radically transform the world and will 'make all things new'. Even if we were to find historical proofs – supposing we had the signed and sealed statements of witnesses, or found archeological evidence for the empty tomb – would we believe? Would we be born again to a living hope? We should probably simply say, 'oh, really?', pigeon-hole the facts that were new to us – and go on living as we did before.

But it becomes quite a different matter if we stop looking at Christ's resurrection in the perspective of history and look at history in the perspective of the resurrection. Then we sense that the compulsion of evil has been broken. Life is stronger than death. And then we shall find the familiar way of the world incomprehensible. First of all we begin to suffer from it, and then to hope for its final conversion – its reversal – its new beginning. Faith does not mean registering a fact called 'the resurrection'. Faith means experiencing the creative power of God, who makes the impossible reality. Faith means rising up out of indolence and joylessness, and participating in the resurrection process. Christ's resurrection is God's way of giving us new life. Being born again to hope is the way in which we acknowledge Christ.

When we see history in the perspective of Christ's resurrection, we have to come back to the saying about 'rebirth'. For a long time this was a forgotten word in the Protestantism of the established churches, which people were 'born into'. The New Testament does not often use the actual word 'rebirth' either, though what the word means is what is intended with every baptism. Matthew 19.28 talks first of all about the *rebirth – palingenesia – of the whole cosmos*, when the Son of man will come with the kingdom of his glory. Hope for rebirth is therefore world-wide and cosmic. It is only in the Epistle to Titus (3.5) that we hear about the *rebirth of believers* according to the mercy of God through Christ in the Holy Spirit. They already become the heirs of eternal life here and now, in hope. The universal expectation of the rebirth of the cosmos, which we find in Matthew, is already experienced by believers *now* in their own lives, according to the Epistle to Titus. The rebirth of an individual person is nothing less than an anticipation of the rebirth of the whole creation. That is the enduring reason why the new life of believers is determined or defined by an inviting hope for the whole of creation, which includes others as well. The new life of hope is not determined by an exclusive hope. It is not that someone simply hopes to save himself and people like him, and lets the rest of the world go to hell. Anyone who is born again to hope sees a future for the whole world, not just for himself. That is why he cannot give up a single person or a single part of life. In Christoph Blumhardt's words: 'If I had to give up hope for a single individual or a single fragment of creation, then for me Christ would not have been raised.'

So the rebirth of our small, unimportant human life is

linked with the divine future for the whole of creation. In this way it gives our transitory life a permanent significance. Our life becomes the sign of hope for the future of the whole world. We ourselves become hope – God's hope in this world. Anyone who understands that is no longer tormented by the question about meaning. He is full of joy and has his hands full with communicating his own hope and passing it on to others.

### (b) *Life in the liberty of the risen Christ*

Christian faith is essentially faith in the resurrection. Faith in the resurrection means being born again to hope. At Taizé the life that springs from this faith was called 'an endless feast'. 'The risen Christ makes life a continual festival, a festival without end', said Athanasius.

'Is it possible to celebrate life in the midst of death?' asked an Argentinian friend, in a letter written at Christmas 1978. 'For those of us who live in Latin America the question isn't an empty phrase. Here we do not only meet death in the context of subversive violence and repressive counter-measures. It surrounds us in a far crueller way in the form of growing unemployment, the decline in the real value of the wages of the poorest of the poor, and in the increase in child mortality.' Is it possible honestly to celebrate the victory of Christ, or to see life as a festival, in a world like this? For so many people, victory seems to be swallowed up in death, and hell seems triumphant.

Faith in the resurrection does not look past death to eternity. Nor does it come to melancholy terms with this vale of tears. It sees the raising of the tortured and crucified Son of Man as *God's great protest* against death and against everyone who plays into death's hands and threatens life. For faith senses that the event of Christ's self-giving and his resurrection reflect God's infinite passion for life, and for the salvation and liberty of his creation. Faith shares this passion. It

31

shares in God's protest, by rising up out of the apathy of misery (and even more out of the cynicism of prosperity) and by fighting against death in the midst of life. Death is the evil power already existing in life's midst, not just at its end. Here is the economic death of the starving, there the political death of the oppressed. Here is the social death of the handicapped; there the noisy death through bombs; and here again the silent death of petrified souls. The raising of Christ is proved by our courage to rise against death. That is not just a play on words. We show our hope for the life that defeats death in our protest against the manifold forms of death in the midst of life. It is only in the passion for life and our giving of ourselves for its liberation that we entrust ourselves utterly to the God who raises the dead.

Faith in the resurrection shows that it is alive when people protest against death. But the resurrection faith itself lives from something different. It lives from the exuberant rapture of God's promised future. It shows its power in resistance. But it lives from measureless astonishment over the future, in the infinite joy of looking towards the new heaven and the new earth, in which righteousness will dwell, and towards eternal blessedness. 'How much more', says the apostle Paul, when he has ceased to talk about *liberation from* sin, law and death, and is talking about *freedom for* eternal life. 'How much more' is the 'added value' of hope, the surplus of promise beyond this life. The 'notwithstanding' with which we resist death and inertia is only the dark side of the shield whose reverse is the 'how much more' of the hope by which we are quickened.

If God's protest against death is to be experienced in the struggle against the forces of death, how and where are we to experience this 'added value', this surplus of hope? It is experienced in 'the feast'. Easter is a feast and is celebrated as the feast of freedom. For Easter is the beginning of the laughter of the redeemed and the dance of the liberated and the creative game of fantasy. Since earliest times Easter hymns have celebrated the victory of life by laughing at death, by mocking at hell, and by making the lords of this world absurd. Easter is God's protest against death. Easter is the feast of freedom from death. We must keep the two things together. Resistance is the protest of those who hope and hope is the festival of those who resist.

(c) *In the expectation of Christ's parousia*
Christ is our hope because Christ is our future. That means that we are waiting and hoping for his second coming, praying 'Come, Lord Jesus, come to the world, come to us!' Just as the resurrection faith is hope's foundation, so Christ's second coming defines hope's horizon. Without the expectation of Christ's second coming there is no Christian hope; for without it hope is not putting its trust in a radical alternative to this world's present condition.

Was it not a sign of Christianity's growing middle-class respectability when expectation of the parousia lost its power – when it was suppressed and subjected to 'enlightened' interpretations, and then emigrated to the so-called 'sects' in the religious underworld of bourgeois society? It is only the person who does not really look for a truly new beginning, or who thinks that he has no need of it, who can do without the alternative future offered by the image of the returning Christ. A person like this can do without this new future. But for the person who commits himself unreservedly to the new beginning, Christ's second coming and messianic kingdom is important. He needs the support of this future if he is to free himself from the present in order to encounter that same present freely. For him, Christ's future is more important than the world's present. That is why he prays, 'let thy kingdom come and the world pass away.'

Admittedly, our translation 'second coming' for the expectation of Christ's parousia and his kingdom is an unlucky

one. It implies that Christ is not there at the moment, but
that he will come again. But this does not correspond to the
experience of his presence in the Spirit. For that reason I find
the old translation used by Luther and Paul Gerhardt better:
they talked about 'the future of Jesus Christ' – and his future
presupposes his *present* and his *presence* in the here and now.

In history, and also among different present-day Christian
groups, the expectation of Christ's future has been linked
with the most widely differing motives. Expectation of the
coming Christ can certainly not be a dream of revenge on
the part of people who have come off badly in this world
('the day of revenge will come!'). Nor can it be a dream of
power on the part of the powerless ('then we shall be the
rulers and our enemies will be destroyed'). Nor, finally, can
it well be a compensation for the disappointed ('things will
be better in heaven'). Expectation and prayer for Christ's
future is none of these things. It is the completion of that
hope which was born of Christ's resurrection. The risen
Christ 'must reign' until he has put all his enemies under his
feet. That is the basis of the apostle's hope for the parousia
(I Cor. 15.25). But if Christ was raised for our justification,
and if he rules through the freedom for which he has set us
free, then we can expect nothing less, and nothing other, of
his future than the fulfilment of justification and a kingdom
of freedom which will also include the whole 'groaning
creation'.

Of course it is true that expectation of Christ's coming in
glory includes the expectation of judgment: 'from thence he
shall come to judge the quick and the dead.' The ending of
evil is part of the consummation of salvation. God's kingdom
involves his judgment. There is no reason to leave this out,
or to keep quiet about it, or to demythologize it, as just being
part of the apocalyptic expectations of an earlier age. But
there is even less reason for being overcome by anxiety or
panic at the thought of the Last Judgment, or for visualizing

it in terms of the horrifying visions of hell we see in medieval pictures. Even the coming judgment of the living and the dead is a subject for *hope*, for longing and the prayer, 'Come soon, Lord Jesus!' For who is the judge? It is the same Christ who gave himself up to death for sinners and who has borne our griefs and sicknesses. How should we not trust ourselves joyfully to his judgment? What will the crucified Jesus judge us by? The law, or his own gospel? Our own acts, or his sufferings for us? How should we not hasten joyfully to meet the universal judge when he is the one who was crucified for us? And finally – what will be the purpose of his judgment? The punishment of the wicked and the reward of the good? Or will his intention be to establish his righteousness everywhere and in everyone? Will he judge us in order to annihilate us, or to save us – to cast us down, or to raise us up? Does the Last Judgment know any other kind of divine righteousness and justice than what we experience here and now in the justification of sinners? The expectation of the Last Judgment ought not to become a projection of our suppressed guilt and anxiety. But neither can it be a projection of our notorious self-justification. It is only when it is based on the remembrance and present experience of Christ that judgment points in the direction of *his* future. His righteousness will triumph! He, the crucified Jesus, will judge! He will judge according to his gospel! The proclamation of the coming judgment is a joyful and liberating message, not a threatening and frightening one. That is why we sing Advent hymns. We can hope just as joyfully for Christ's judgment as for his kingdom. Whatever may happen and whoever we may be – it is our Lord who comes. Thanks be to God!

## 5  *Called to Hope*

There is an old Jewish story in the Talmud. A rabbi was considering what questions a Jew would probably have to answer at the Last Judgment. What would the universal judge ask? First of all the rabbi thought of the obvious things: Were you honest in business? Did you seek wisdom? Did you keep the commandments? and so on. Finally a question came into his mind which surprised the rabbi himself. It was the question about the Messiah. The universal judge will ask, 'Did you hope for my Messiah?' For the messianic expectation is an essential part of the Jew's experience of faith.

If the Christian faith is essentially hope, then Christians too will realize that when the Lord comes he will ask them, 'Did you hope for me? Did you go on hoping to the end? Did you keep hoping even when you nearly gave up? Did you fall away? Did you endure to the end?' His questions about our hope and our remaining in hope are important – so important that our eternal salvation depends on the answer: he that endures to the end shall be saved. In the hope that abides we abide too and do not pass away. In abiding hope we trust in Christ's victory and do not yield it up to joylessness. We do not yield his victory to evil.

> We are called to hope!
> Let us go forth from our anxieties
> and learn to hope from the Bible.
> Let us reach out beyond our limitations
> in order to find a future in a new beginning.
> Let us take no more account of barriers,
> but only of the one who broke the barriers down.
> He is risen.
> Christ is risen indeed.
> He is our future.

# Anxiety

A year or two ago, in 1978, there were two major analyses of the situation in West Germany, one made in the United States and the other in England. Both these analyses came to the same conclusion. They decided that the most striking German characteristic was no longer frantic industriousness, or the self-complacent 'German economic miracle', or even the much admired stability of the German mark. The main characteristic was anxiety. It was not anxiety about any particular thing. It was a general malaise, a loss of confidence – an undefined attitude to life which continually expects the worst. To find anxiety of this kind as the chief characteristic of an economically stable country is a remarkable phenomenon. But is certainly not a phenomenon that is peculiar to Germany alone. Today all the wealthy countries of the world are dominated by anxiety. There is a general loss of bearings and a widespread feeling of demoralization.

The 60s were an era of hope and protest all over the world. The 70s were a period of anxiety and self-pity everywhere in our affluent society. 'The Age of Anxiety' was the name W. H. Auden gave to the powerful poem in which he evokes the hopelessness of 'the lost generation' in the last war. And we are living in that age of anxiety today.

There are certainly reasons enough for our anxiety.

Which country can overcome the energy crisis?

What about the dangers of nuclear energy?

What work is going to be left for men and women, and who will be able to find a job, in our computerized age?

How can we solve the hunger and over-population of the Third World? We have done nothing decisive about it at all in the last twenty years. Isn't our anxiety about these impoverished people prompted by guilt?

Yet, frightening though these questions are, our anxiety has a much deeper origin. We are anxious about the future, but it is our very anxiety that is robbing us of the confidence we need to master its problems. Anxiety blurs vision and judgment. We are paralysed by our anxiety and, like a rabbit paralysed by a snake, our very fear is our doom. In anxiety our minds and hearts already experience what we are afraid of. And this means that anxiety is seldom a helpful guide for our decisions and actions.

Psychologically, however, there is something even more dangerous than anxiety about the future, and that is anxiety about anxiety, the fear of fear. We are very well aware that anxiety makes us impotent; so we are afraid of fear even before we feel it. Because we are afraid of our fear, we react to the threatening situations we meet hysterically and aggressively. If we are afraid of fear we repress our feelings. This fear of fear is the really infantile and dangerous thing about anxiety. It makes us afraid of ourselves, not just of the future. It makes us feel that we do not know ourselves and cannot trust ourselves.

If we are to survive in an age of anxiety, we have to face the experience of anxiety with the courage of hope, but also with patience. We cannot remove all the objective reasons for our anxiety. But we can overcome our fear of fear by beginning to search our own hearts and by learning to know ourselves in the experience of anxiety and under its pressures. No one is ever totally free of anxiety. To be so would mean being a superman – but also completely inhuman. But we can learn to live with anxiety, to accept it, and to be free under its pressures. Of course we must do our utmost to eliminate the situations and conditions that make us anxious, but we cannot do away with anxiety itself. We have to accept it as a subjective experience, endure it, and transform it.

But *can* the destructive force of anxiety be transformed into a positive and vital power? I believe that the Christian faith shows us that even this is possible.

## 1  Anxiety and Hope

One of Grimm's Fairy Tales is 'the story of the boy who went out to learn how to be afraid'. He went through the most dangerous adventures, totally unimpressed, finding nothing frightening about them. He knew neither fear nor dread. Then one night, in order to cure him, his loving wife tipped a bucket of cold water, full of prickly little fish, over him as he slept. He was seized by a nameless horror and panic in which he seemed like a stranger to himself.

Two modern thinkers, a theologian and a philosopher, have picked up this story and have drawn very different conclusions from it.

In *The Concept of Dread* Sören Kierkegaard used the story as a starting-point for what he wanted to say:

One of Grimm's Fairy Tales is a story about a lad who went out to seek adventure in order to learn how to shiver with fear. We will let the adventurer go his ways without concerning ourselves further about whether he met horror as he went or not. What I should like to say here is that this is an adventure which everyone has to face: the adventure of learning *how to be afraid*, so as not to be lost, either through not having learnt how to fear, or through being completely engulfed by anxiety. The person who has learnt how to be afraid in the right way has learnt the most important thing of all.[1]

Ernst Bloch began his *Prinzip Hoffnung* ('the principle of hope') with what is apparently the contrary view:

Once upon a time a man went out in order to learn how to be afraid. That was easier to do in times past, when fear was always close at hand. The art of being afraid was something people were terribly proficient in. But now, except where there are real reasons for fear, a more appropriate feeling is expected of us.

The important thing now is *to learn how to hope*. The labour of hope never gives anything up. Hope is in love with success, not with failure. Hope is above fear. It is not passive like fear; even less is it locked away into pure Nothingness. The emotion of hope goes out from itself. It expands men and women, instead of limiting them and hedging them in . . .[2]

Learning to be afraid and learning to hope are contrasted with one another here. But are they really contrasts?

Of course the person who is forced into a tight corner becomes afraid, while hope opens up vision and outlook. Anxiety – *anxietas* – chokes us. Hope – *spes* – lets us breathe. Anxiety weakens us and makes us small and mean. But the person who is strengthened by hope can raise his head and learn to walk upright. We are afraid of imprisonment and death. But hope longs for life and liberty. So would it not be better to learn how to hope with Ernst Bloch, rather than to learn how to be afraid with Kierkegaard? At first glance everyone would immediately agree that hope is above fear. Hope can lead to anxiety. Anxiety cannot lead to hope. But by seizing on fear and hope as simple alternatives, have we really grasped the deeper significance of these two attitudes?

What anxiety and hope actually have in common is a sense of what is possible.[3] In anxiety we anticipate possible danger. In hope we anticipate possible deliverance. Of course it is true that in his anxiety a person always envisages the worst, and his terrified imaginings increase his anxiety. But without the feeling of fear and anxiety he would not notice the danger at all. Without anxiety we would be blind, ruthless and careless. In anxiety and hope we go beyond existing reality and anticipate *the future*, so as to make a correct decision about the present. How could we *hope* for life, liberty and happiness, and snatch hopefully at the chances of these things which the future offers, if we did not simultaneously *fear* death, oppression and misfortune? 'The future' is as ambiguous as potentiality itself. For the world process has not yet been finally decided. Consequently the future means both opportunity and danger. It fills us with enthusiasm and threatens us at the same time. And if this is so, how can we learn to hope without also learning to be afraid? Even if 'hope is above fear' as Bloch says, anxiety is still the inescapable and self-evident sister of hope. We cannot learn to hope if we suppress our anxiety and shut our eyes to danger. On the other hand, we must also ask ourselves whether anyone has ever learnt how to be anxious unless he has first gone out of himself in hope and lived in hope. Can anyone know what anxiety is if he does not venture to hope for anything? If a person has to learn how to be afraid, as Kierkegaard says, he needs an even greater hope, if he is not to be numbed by anxiety or totally engulfed by it. When we look towards the open future, obscure and undetermined as it is, it is hope which gives us courage; yet it is anxiety that makes us circumspect and cautious – which gives us foresight. So how can hope become wise without anxiety? Courage without caution is rash. But caution without courage makes people hesitant and leaden-footed. In this respect 'the concept of dread' and 'the principle of hope' are not opposites after all; they are complementary and mutually dependent.

Kierkegaard and Bloch agree about one thing: that anxiety and hope *can both be learnt*. This common assertion is an astonishing one, for we are inclined to ask in our fatalistic way: how can we do anything about our anxieties? And surely hope is a pure gift of grace – and a rare gift at that?

If, in spite of what we have always supposed, anxiety and hope are *learnable*, then someone must show us how we can – and must – learn them both. The story of the boy who went out to learn how to be afraid is an exodus story. It is the story of someone who leaves his home and everything that life has meant for him up to now in order to find freedom. Without an exodus of this kind out of what has been until now, into an unknown, adventurous future, there is no way of learning how to hope or how to fear. Every adventure is a journey of hope, and yet something of a nightmare at the same time. In this sense the whole of life is an adventure, a risk, continual hope and continual anxiety. The exodus out of existing reality into the potentialities of the future is the road to freedom.[4] It is on this road that we 'learn' how to be anxious and how to hope. Anxiety and hope seem to me to be the two sides of the experience of freedom. Anyone who wants to experience freedom must be prepared for anxiety and yet for hope as well – be prepared to hope, and just because of that be prepared to be anxious too.

## 2  The Anxiety of Christ

All human anxiety and fear is fundamentally – which means from birth onwards – fear of separation. Fear makes us lonely. Fear isolates us. Fear strikes us dumb. Does fear and anxiety also isolate us from the foundation of our being, from the meaning of life, from God? Normally the gods know no anxiety, for they exist, independent of any changing destiny, in some world beyond life and death, in eternal bliss. If this is what divine eternity is like, however, then anxiety also isolates men and women from their gods, making their lives godless and meaningless. But then is not a person who is capable of anxiety and hope, because he is also capable of love, greater than all the gods who know neither anxiety nor hope because they cannot love?

> For the loving worm within its clod,
> Were diviner than a loveless God
> Amid his worlds, I would dare to say.[5]

If we believe in Christ fear does not isolate us from God. On the contrary, it leads us deeper into fellowship with him. Christian faith in God is essentially fellowship with Christ, and fellowship with Christ is essentially fellowship with the Christ who was tempted and assailed, who suffered and was forsaken. In our anxiety we participate in Christ's anxiety; for in his suffering Christ went through the very fears and anxieties which men and women encounter too.[6]

In Christian devotion the crucified Jesus has always brought consolation in anxiety and fear. And this is certainly not because Christ, as God's Son, was by nature a Christ who was able to live free of anxiety and suffering. He is our consolation just because of his 'agony and bloody sweat' – just because he shrank from every lash and felt the prick of every thorn. Paul Gerhardt's passion hymn brings this out particularly vividly:

> And when my heart must languish
> Amidst the final throe,
> Release me from mine anguish
> By thine own pain and woe.[7]

All we have to say as Christians about 'religiously integrated anxiety' and the way to overcome anxiety is to be found in this verse. We have to be 'released' from anxiety. We cannot 'get the better of it' by ourselves. And we are released from it, not through the divine omnipotence of a heavenly Christ, but through Christ's earthly and most profoundly human suffering and fear. 'Only the suffering God can help us', wrote Dietrich Bonhoeffer from his prison cell;

and Kierkegaard too goes on, after the passage we have quoted, to talk of Christ 'who was in dread even unto death'. But this means that we are released from our anxieties through Christ's. We are released from our suffering through his. Our wounds, paradoxically, are healed by other wounds, as Isaiah 53 promises of the Servant of God.

Let us consider two biblical passages, which can help us to grasp the mystery of anxiety and fear in Christian faith. Let us think first about Christ's anxiety in Gethsemane, and then about his agony on Golgotha. Then we shall go on to consider the truth of the suffering God, who can console men and women in their anxiety and fear.

## (a) Gethsemane

Christ's passion does not just begin when he is taken prisoner and tortured by the Roman soldiers. It begins at the moment when he resolves to go to Jerusalem with his disciples. His passion for the messianic future, which he had brought to living expression in the gospel for the poor, in the healing of the sick and the forgiveness of sins, was bound to come up against its most determined enemies in Jerusalem; for its strongest opponents were the priests of Jesus' own people and the Roman forces of occupation. So the threat that 'the Son of man must suffer many things, and be rejected' (Mark 8.31) hung heavy over the road to Jerusalem.

When he entered into the holy city the people recognized him and cried, 'Hosanna! Blessed is he who comes in the name of the Lord! Blessed is the kingdom of our father David that is coming!' (Mark 11.9f.). They saw in Jesus the messianic kingdom and greeted his appearance with this expectation. This makes the reaction of the Jewish authorities and the occupying forces all the more understandable: the man from Nazareth is dangerous. He must disappear, quickly and without more ado. Up to now there has been nothing unusual about the story. Everyone is prepared to accept suffering for some great passion – even to sacrifice his life for it if need be. But in Christ's case a different kind of suffering was involved as well.

The night before he was arrested he went into the garden of Gethsemane, taking three of his disciples with him, and 'began to be greatly distressed and troubled', writes Mark. 'He began to be sorrowful and troubled', records Matthew. 'My soul is very sorrowful, even to death', he says, and begs his friends to stay awake with him. Earlier, too he had often withdrawn at nights, in order to be united in the innermost prayer of his heart with the God to whom he always gave the exclusive name of 'my Father'. But in Gethsemane for the first time he does not want to be alone with God. He is afraid of him. That is why he looks to his friends to protect him. Then comes the prayer which in its original version sounds like a demand: 'Father, all things are possible to thee; remove this cup from me' (Mark 14.35) – spare me this suffering. Matthew and Luke soften the Gethsemane prayer into something more modest: 'If it be possible' or 'if Thou art willing' 'let this cup pass from me'.[8]

What suffering is meant by 'the cup'? God does not hear his Son's prayer. He rejects it. Elsewhere the gospel tells us: 'I and the Father are one.' But here the Father withdraws from the Son, leaving him alone. It is the cup of separation. That is why, exhausted by grief, the disciples fall into a deep sleep. It is only in the 'nevertheless' which is in such total contradiction to what he desires that Christ holds fast to the fellowship with the God who as Father withdraws from him: 'Nevertheless not as I will, but as Thou wilt.' Christ had to learn obedience through the prayer which God rejected.

Christ's real passion begins with this unanswered prayer. This is the beginning of his fear and suffering as he endured the experience of being forsaken by God. Of course it was also quite simply fear of a slow and horrible death. It would be ridiculous to say that, as the Son of God, he would have been unable to experience the fear of death because his soul lived in unbroken enjoyment of divine power and bliss; and that it was only in the body that he suffered (though this is what Augustine maintained). But it would also be foolish to see him as a morbidly sensitive person who was overcome by self-pity at the prospect of the torments of death awaiting him, as in *Jesus Christ, Superstar*. In the fear that laid hold of him and lacerated his soul, what he suffered from was God. Abandonment by God is the 'cup' which does not pass from him. The appalling silence of the Father in response to the Son's prayer in Gethsemane is more than the silence of death. Martin Buber called it 'the eclipse of God'. It is echoed in 'the dark night of the soul' of the mystics. The Father withdraws and God is silent. This is the experience of hell and judgment.

Luther reinterpreted the traditional doctrine of Christ's 'descent into hell', relating it to his agony from Gethsemane to Golgotha. The nadir of Christ's humiliation was this experience of being forsaken by God. 'Not only in the eyes of the world and his disciples, nay, even in his own eyes did Christ see himself as lost, as forsaken by God, felt in his conscience that he was cursed by God – suffered the torment of the damned who feel God's eternal wrath, shrink back from it and flee.' This was how he interpreted the passion of the assailed and tempted Christ, the Christ who was assailed and tempted by God.[9] Consequently, for Luther Christ was far from the superstar, the most perfect man; he was the most tempted, and therefore the most miserable of all. Moreover he was not only assailed by fear and suffering in his human nature, as scholastic tradition maintained. He was assailed in his very essence, in his relationship to the Father – in his divine Sonship.[10] In his Bible Luther headed this chapter 'The struggle in Gethsemane'. It was Christ's struggle with God. This is where the abyss of his anxiety is to be found. He overcomes this agony by surrendering himself to his abandonment by God. That is where we find his victory.

## (b) Golgotha

The other story is to be found at the end of Christ's passion. Again it is a prayer or, to be more precise, the desparing cry of accusation with which Christ dies: 'My God, why hast thou forsaken me?' (Mark 15.34). He hung on the cross for three hours, waiting to die, his limbs and muscles apparently locked in tetanus. Then he died with a cry welling up from a sense of the most profound rejection by the God whose Son he knew himself to be, and whose messianic kingdom had been his whole passion.

This must surely be the historical kernel of the Golgotha story; for the idea that the Saviour's last words to God his Father could possibly have been this outburst of abandonment could never have taken root in the Christian faith if they had never been spoken, or if this abandonment had never been perceptible from Christ's death cry.

Yet we ourselves cannot get used to the fact that this cry of the forsaken Christ stands at the centre of the Christian faith. The history of tradition shows that the horror and dismay emanating from this cry was later softened down, and Christ's utterance was replaced by more pious parting words – for example Luke's 'Into thy hands I commend my spirit'. Nor is the cry made more acceptable to us because it is the opening of Psalm 22, and according to Jewish custom the beginning stands for the whole psalm. For one thing the psalm ends with a glorious prayer of thanksgiving for deliverance from death – and there was no deliverance on Golgotha. For another, after a short time the crucified Jesus was probably incapable of speech. Early manuscripts of Mark's gospel express the cry of abandonment even more drastically: 'Why hast thou given me up to shame?' and 'Why hast thou cursed me?' Even the Epistle to the Hebrews, which was written much later, holds fast to this remembrance of the assailed and forsaken Christ when it says that 'far from God' (perhaps rather 'without God') 'he tasted death for us all' (Heb. 2.9).[11] It is surely not by chance, either, that this cry is the only time Christ does not call God familiarly 'my Father' but addresses him out of the infinite remoteness of separation as 'my God'.

What he was afraid of, what he struggled with in Gethsemane, and what he implored the Father to save him from, happened on the cross. The Father forsook him, delivering him up to the fear of hell. The one who knew himself to be the Son is forsaken, rejected and cursed. And God is silent. With profound insight, Paul interpreted this as meaning that from Gethsemane to Golgotha Christ suffered God's judgment, in which everyone is alone and against which no man can stand: 'For our sake he made him to be sin' (II Cor. 5.21) and 'He became a curse for us' (Gal. 3.13).

### 3 'Release us from our anguish'

If Christ's pain and suffering come from his experience of God at Gethsemane and Golgotha, how can they 'release' the believer from his distress, as Paul Gerhardt says in his hymn? The two different ideas can be traced in the history of faith; and again we find them especially in the young Luther: the idea of the Christ who suffers *with* us, and the idea of the Christ who suffers *for* us. Christ our brother in anxiety and fear, and Christ our representative in our time of need.

(*a*) The first of these ideas says: whatever pain, weakness and loneliness people experience in the fear and anxiety of separation, culminates in the experience of being forsaken by God. It is this that lies behind the anxiety which goes beyond anything definable and finite and which therefore threatens our own identity so hellishly. What Christ experienced in his fear in Gethsemane is the crystallization of this measureless anxiety, which – consciously or unconsciously – lies heavy on the hearts of us all. He is the most assailed of all, for he suffered anxiety in its godless depths and did not flee from it. He suffered the fear of being forsaken by God which all the rest of us can feel but which we do not really have to endure. Anyone who has this sense of being forsaken by God in his fear experiences 'godly grief' (II Cor. 7.10), the divine sorrow. He participates in Christ's anxiety because Christ has borne – and borne alone – the very same anxiety he feels. In his anxiety he conforms to the forsaken Christ. In the image of the crucified Jesus our indefinable anxiety takes on a form with which we can identify ourselves because in that image we discover our own total misery. It is a part of ourselves, our own identity, our own grief. This is the conformity christology which determined the Luther renaissance of the 20s. It is the christology of the 'Christ with us', of Christ our brother, who is our companion on the path through fear, temptation, imprisonment, exile and abandonment by God himself. Through the writings of Jochem Klepper and Heinrich Vogel, this christology saved the souls and lives of many men and women in the fears and anxieties of the Second World War and the post-war period. But it had found its best expression a long time before, in Paul Gerhardt's great Easter hymn, *Auf, auf, mein Herz* whose identification between the believer and Christ[12] was, for English readers, later echoed so closely by Charles Wesley:

> Made like Him, like Him we rise;
> Ours the cross, the grave, the skies.

The other idea, which is inextricably linked with the first, is Christ's vicarious suffering of fear and pain. He suffered for us 'and for many'; he stands in our place. Wherever, after

Easter, Paul and the Epistle to the Hebrews talk about the suffering of Christ, they never forget to add the interpretative words 'for us'. Christ's sufferings have meaning for our sufferings today. But the words also bring out the uniqueness and unrepeatability of Christ's suffering and pain. Easter happened only once. The believer is not merely brought into solidarity with Christ's fate. He also, and even more, enters into a relationship of gratitude, liberated from fear. For the knowledge that another has gone through everything that threatens me and which I was afraid of, is for me a liberation. It liberates me from my fear of fear. The knowledge that the suffering Christ takes my place and surrenders himself for my sake to the abyss of anxiety where he is abandoned by God, frees me from my own anxiety; for it gives me an indestructible identity in my fellowship with him. The knowledge that Christ stands in my place 'releases' me from anxiety, so that I can leave it behind me and its threatening power collapses. But this knowledge also frees me to look at my fear squarely, and to cease being afraid of it. That is why gratitude for the fear Christ suffered is a theme of all the passion hymns:

> Were the whole realm of nature mine,
> That were an offering far too small.[13]

Christ suffers with us and Christ suffers for us. The two images of Christ belong together. Without the brother in our anxiety there is no fellowship with Christ. Without the Christ who substitutes for us in our anxiety, we cannot be freed from that anxiety.

### 4   The Pain of God

I said earlier that for Luther Christ was not only tortured by fear and pain in his human nature, but suffered as Son of God – that is to say in his relationship to the Father. This points to a truth which, when we perceive it, is terrifying and yet consoling. It is the truth of *the suffering God* who encompasses human suffering and so abolishes the anxiety tormenting men and women.

Inspired by Kierkegaard, the Spanish philosopher and poet Miguel de Unamuno brought out this perception in his book *The Tragic Sense of Life.*

God is revealed to us because he suffers and because we suffer; because he suffers he requires our love, and because we suffer he gives us his love, and he envelops our anguish with the eternal and infinite anguish.

All this constituted the scandal of Christianity among the Jews and Greeks, among the Pharisees and the Stoics, and this ancient scandal, the scandal of the cross, is still its scandal and will continue to be so, even among Christians: the scandal of a God who becomes man in order that he may suffer and die, and rise again because he has suffered and died, the scandal of a God who suffers and dies. And this truth, the truth that God suffers, a truth which appalls the mind of man, is the revelation emerging from the very matrix and mystery of the Universe, revealed to us when God sent his Son so that he might redeem us by suffering and dying. It was the revelation of the divinity of suffering, for only that which suffers is divine.[14]

Gazing on the Spanish crucifixes, Unamuno saw Christ's pain as an eternal revelation. God reveals himself in pain; and he reveals his pain.

God suffers in each and all of us, . . . and we all suffer in him. Religious anguish is nought but divine suffering, the feeling that God suffers in me and that I suffer in him.[15]

Unamuno starts from the Spanish cult of the agony of Christ and therefore finds in Christ's inner laceration the revelation of an inner tragedy in God himself. His greatness lay in his not separating God from the crucified Christ, but identifying them. A God who suffers cannot be the cause of suffering, he contains suffering in himself. That is the solution to the problem of evil. Unamuno's limitation is undoubtedly to be found in the fact that through this interpretation the cross becomes God's eternal signature, and fear and suffering are given eternal validity in the form of a fundamentally tragic outlook on life.

Another thinker of the same period, Nikolai Berdyaev, presented the truth of the suffering God similarly in his book *The Meaning of History*.

The divine life itself is history in the profoundest and most mysterious sense. It is a historical drama, a historical mystery play ... because the fate of the crucified Son of God, which is the deepest of all Christian mysteries, is nothing other than the tragic mystery of suffering which the Godhead himself endures.

In God himself there is a thirst for his counterpart, his Other, and a hunger for the freedom of the beloved he has created.

When in the divine life a passion tragedy is played – a particular divine destiny in the centre of which stands the suffering of God himself and of his Son – and if in this suffering the redemption and liberation of the world is fulfilled, then this can only be explained by saying that the profoundest source of such a tragic conflict, such a tragic movement, and such a tragic passion is present in the depths of the divine life itself.[16]

Although Berdyaev does not only talk about a 'tragic attitude to life', but actually, like Jacob Böhme, talks about a tragedy in the objective sense – a dramatic history with God and in God himself – we have to ask here whether the truth about the suffering God is not again being obscured? Whether suffering in the world is not given an eternal permanence? So that man in his suffering and his fear certainly participates in God's pain, but is not released from his own suffering and fear.

We must therefore accept the insights Unamuno and Berdyaev have given us; but we must go beyond them. If we follow the testimony of the first Christian witnesses, the depth of the agony of fear which Christ experienced on the cross is far and away surpassed by the sense of expansion in his resurrection.[17] The experience of suffering over his abandonment by God on Golgotha is far surpassed by his resurrection into the joy of God's coming glory. This means that we must not isolate the cross, let alone make it something absolute in itself. We must not linger in Gethsemane and beneath the cross endlessly repeating what it teaches us of pain and fear. Without the resurrection, the cross really is quite simply a tragedy and nothing more than that. In Latin America the Indians follow the 'stations of the cross' without the feast of Easter liberation; so these processions really do lead to masochism – to self-laceration in a quite literal sense – to a cruel lust for pain, and an intensification of fear.

But according to the faith of the first Christians, Christ's resurrection far surpasses his passion. The cross and the resurrection do not simply balance one another out. 'How much more', Paul often says, when he is talking about grace, or freedom, or the resurrection. So in the end we must after all agree with Ernst Bloch: for the Christian faith too, hope is above fear. The promise we hear in the history of Christ's crucifixion and resurrection is utterly remote from the death wish. It is the call that beckons us to freedom. 'He allured you out of distress into a broad place where there was no cramping' (Job 36.16). But what kind of freedom does this mean? Suppressed anxiety is not sufficient to produce freedom. But anxiety that is given permanent significance does not lead to freedom either. It is only faith that can 'raise anxiety up' – take away what is weakening about it and preserve its cautious foresight. For Christians this becomes evident in the figure of Christ, who was raised to glory from the shameful death on the cross. This path from the cross to the resurrection is Christ's passover, the new exodus into eternal liberty. The anxiety that has been 'raised' and the experience of anxiety which still exists might be called 'blessed anxiety' because it is an anxiety that has been liberated.

If, finally, we sum up the experience of faith in anxiety and fear, this is what we may say:

Our numerous fears and anxieties continually crystallize into a general anxiety about life. It is this heightened and diffused anxiety which spreads, takes on independent existence and robs men and women of their self-confidence and their very identity. It can be described as the fear of fear. It wins the upper hand and drives us into a corner if we fail to identify it for what it is, or if we try to ignore it. Then we feel that our situation is hopeless. We no longer know who we really are.

Christian faith identifies this anxiety with abandonment by God. It is a separation phobia, a dread of separation from the foundation of existence, the meaning of life, what is worthy of trust. To identify anxiety and give it a name is not enough to free us from it, or to let us conquer it.

We have to be 'released' from anxiety. That is the experience of faith in anxiety. When we remember Christ's fear and anxiety, what he has already done with us and for us is repeated: he has endured the fear of being forsaken by God – the fear of separation; and he has opened up a way through this experience for those who trust and follow him. In fellowship with him we discover that we are released from anxiety as we endure it. By recognizing our anxiety in his, and by seeing it as abolished in his, we experience that 'blessed' anxiety which kindles an unconquerable hope. To be 'released' from fear means standing up to fear, resisting it. It means walking freely through the midst of fear, sustained by hope, because nothing 'in the whole creation will be able to separate us from the love of God in Christ Jesus our Lord'.

# The Theology of Mystical Experience

### CONTEMPLATION IN A WORLD OF ACTION

Mystical theology aims at being a wisdom drawn from experience, not a doctrinal wisdom.[1] The theology itself is not mystical. It is only mystical because it tries to express mystical experience in words. But since it is impossible to convey mystical experience itself through doctrinal statements, the theology of mystical experience always only talks about the way, the journey, the voyage out to that unutterable experience of God which no one can tell or communicate. As far as its doctrinal content is concerned, the theology of the mystics has never seemed particularly impressive, even down to the present day. It is easy enough to recognize the Augustinian, and the Neoplatonic, and the gnostic ideas, and to trace them historically back to their roots. But this way of looking at things is not the approach of the mystic theologians themselves. So it is more appropriate to ask what experiences they were trying to express with the help of these particular images and ideas. And if we want to share their experiences, the best thing is to accompany them on their pilgrimage – whether it is with Bernard of Clairvaux on 'the ladder of love', or with Bonaventure on 'the pilgrimage of the soul', or with Thomas à Kempis on the way he called 'the imitation of Christ', or with Theresa of Avila and her 'interior castle', or with Thomas Merton on 'the seven-storey mountain'.

The mystical *sapientia experimentalis* is always ethical and mystical at the same time. It is both teaching about virtue, and a search for new experience; for only the pure in heart shall see God. This does not mean an external division of life into 'knowledge' and 'practice', or religion and ethics. From Augustine onwards, the whole of life has, for the mystics, been the drama of love – unhappy love, despairing love, liberated love, love that seeks, and love that has achieved the bliss it sought for. All the mystics start from the assumption that man is an erotic being. He is possessed by a greedy desire, a Faustian drive, a hungry heart. For the infinite God arouses in his image, man, an infinite passion which destroys everything that is finite and earthly, unless it finds rest in his divine infinity. That is why love's only measure is the immeasurable.[2] We can still trace Augustine's *cor inquietum* – his 'restless heart' – in Marx and Freud. 'Man', said Marx, 'as a realistic, sensual being . . . is a suffering being and – because he feels that he suffers – a passionate one. Passion is the essential power of man to strive earnestly for his object'.[3] What object is it that can satisfy this passion?

What the early and the modern mystics all describe is really the history of the liberation of human passion from the melancholy forms of satisfaction which have so pitifully miscarried. What they describe is really the tragic love affair between God and men. Is this a sentimental way of putting it? It only sounds sentimental if we forget that disappointed love is the most terrible thing we can suffer. It is the power of destruction, a longing for suicide, the fury of annihilation. The mystics have described their paths to the liberation from passion in different ways. I am not going to attempt here to analyse the different 'heavenly journeys of the soul' historically, or to reduce them systematically to a common denominator. I should myself only like to describe a journey of this kind, which leads to this experience, by inviting you to consider the following stages:

1. Action and meditation
2. Meditation and contemplation
3. Contemplation and mystical union
4. Mysticism and discipleship
5. The vision of the world in God.

These are only a few of a whole multitude of stages. The longest journey is always the inward one. The journey home to find oneself takes a whole lifetime; and perhaps more.


## 1 *Action and Meditation*

Ever since 'practice' has been elevated into the criterion of truth, meditation has counted as being useless and untrue, because it is speculative. Since, as Berthold Brecht tells us, truth always has to be concrete, meditation counts as 'abstract'. It is a flight from reality and action. In societies which force men and women into active life, and only reward achievement and success, meditation also counts as being superseded, useless and superfluous. That is understandable enough. What is not understandable is when meditation exercises are recommended to nervy activists and worn-out managers, on the grounds that they provide a useful kind of counterbalancing sport, which will help them to recover their mental equilibrium; or when yoga techniques are sold as a means of increasing performance. Pragmatic and utilitarian marketing means the final destruction of meditation. It does not let people find peace, and even if they find peace they do not find themselves in the process.

Meditation is really a very ancient method of acquiring knowledge, which has only been pushed aside by our modern activism. Meditation is a mode of perception which we continually practise in everyday life, without noticing it particularly, and without surrendering ourselves to it. We see that a tree is beautiful, for example – and drive past it at 50 mph. Or we become aware of ourselves, in the moment between night and dawn – and hurry off to work, forgetting ourselves altogether. We have no time to be aware of things, or of ourselves. Why not?

When we try to get to know something by the methods of modern science, we know in order to achieve mastery, to dominate. *Scientia est potestas*, said Francis Bacon, 'knowledge is power'. For by means of science we take possession of the object, becoming what Descartes promised the scientist would become – *maître et possesseur de la nature*, the master and possessor of nature. And then nature becomes mute. That is why modern reason has been made operational: it 'knows only that which it brings forth according to its own design', as Kant says. Knowledge is production. Nothing else? No, practically nothing else. Reason is a productive organ, but hardly a perceptive one. Meditation, on the other hand, is pre-eminently a way of perceiving, of receiving, of absorbing and participating.

We can make this difference clear to ourselves if we think of it in the following way. It is by no means true that we comprehend the world solely through the 'little grey cells' of our brain. We always draw on our senses as well. What senses do we use in order to acquire understanding and knowledge?

The Greek philosophers, the Fathers of the church and the monastic Fathers comprehended things with their eyes. They literally 'theorized' (θεωρεῖν = 'to look at'). We really arrive at understanding when we go on looking at a flower or a sunset or a manifestation of God until we recognize in *this* flower the flower *per se*; and in *this* sunset, *the* sunset; and until we see in *this* manifestation of God, God in his entirety and nothing but God himself. Then the observer himself becomes part of the flower, or part of the sunset, or part of God. For he participates in his object or counterpart through his perception, and is transported into it. The act of perception transforms the perceiver, not what is perceived. Perception confers communion. We perceive in order to participate, not in order to dominate. That is why we can only perceive to the extent in which we are capable of loving what we see (in Augustine's words, *tantum cognoscitur, quantum diligitur*). Knowledge, as the Hebrew word tells us, is an act of love, not an act of domination. When someone has understood, he says: 'I see it. I love you. I behold God.' The result is pure theory (θεωρία).

Today we understand things differently, for we understand *with our hands*: we want to *grasp* everything. We acquire knowledge with our touching, grasping, conquering, possessing and colonizing hands. In German the word for knowing (*kennen*) is etymologically linked, significantly enough, with the word which means being able to *do* something (*können*). 'Knowing' means 'know-how'. And 'understanding' means understanding how to do something. If we have 'grasped' something, we also have it *in our grasp*. It is under our control; we possess it. If we possess something, we can do what we like with it. So we know in order to dominate. If someone thinks he understands something, he says, 'Yes, I grasp that; I've got it; I can cope with it'. The result is pure domination.

If we compare these two ways of knowing, it is easy to see that modern men and women need at least a balance between active and contemptive life, if they are not to atrophy spiritually. The pragmatic way of grasping things has very obvious limits, and beyond these limits the destruction of life begins. This applies not only to our dealings with other people, but also to our dealings with the natural environment.

But the meditative way of understanding seems to be even more important when it is applied to a person's dealings with his own self. We find flight into special action and practical political activism, because people cannot endure what they themselves are. They have 'fallen out' with themselves. This means that they cannot stand being alone. Loneliness is torture. Silence is unendurable. Solitude is already felt to be 'social death'. Every disappointment becomes the frustration which has to be avoided at all costs. But the person who throws himself into practical life because he cannot come to terms with himself, simply becomes a burden for other people. Social activism and political involvement are not a remedy for the weakness of our own personalities. Anyone who wants to act on the behalf of other people without having deepened his own understanding of himself, without having built up his capacity for sensitive loving, and without having found self-confidence and freedom towards himself, will find nothing in himself that he can give to anyone else. Even presupposing good will and the lack of evil intentions, he will still only pass on to them the infection of his own egoism, the aggressions caused by his own anxiety, and the prejudices of his own ideology. Anyone who wants to fill up his own hollowness by helping other people will only spread that very same hollowness. Why? Because people are far less influenced by what another person says and does than the activist would like to believe; they are influenced by the other person's own *being*, by what he is. Only the person who has found his own self can give of his own self. What else can he give? It is only the person who knows that he is accepted who can accept others without dominating them. The person who has become free in himself can liberate others and share their suffering.

This is not meant as a criticism of social and political activity as such. On the contrary, this activity is only strengthened by the self-awareness we have described. For it is only the person who has discovered a stable identity in himself who will protest against social injustice and resist political oppression and be prepared to make the necessary sacrifices. What inner strength do we require in order to 'become a stranger to our brethren'?

It is a remarkable fact that when, in modern novels, for instance, the misery of people with weak personalities is described it is always the key words of mysticism that are used. But what are virtues for the mystic are torment and sickness for the modern man or woman: estrangement, loneliness, silence, solitude, inner emptiness, deprivation, poverty, not-knowing, and so forth. We only have to think of the wretchedness depicted in Ingmar Bergman's films, to see how mysticism can turn into nihilism. What the monks sought for in order to find God, modern men and women fly from as if it were the devil. Earlier, mystics withdrew into the loneliness of the desert in order to fight with demons and to experience Christ's victory over them. It seems to me that today we need people who are prepared to enter into the inner wilderness of the soul and wander through the abysses of the self in order to fight with demons, and to experience Christ's victory there; or simply in order to make an inner space for living possible, and to open up a way of escape for other people through spiritual experience. And in our context this means: wresting a positive meaning out of the loneliness, the silence, the inner emptiness, the suffering, the poverty, the spiritual dryness and 'the knowledge that knows nothing'. The mystics experienced this meaning in the form of a paradox. For them it meant learning to live in the absence of the God who is present, or in the presence of the God who is absent, and enduring what St John of the Cross called 'the dark night of the soul'. Can it still mean that today?

## 2  Meditation and Contemplation

There are many definitions of meditation and contemplation, and many distinctions have been made between the two.[4]

For my own practical purposes I would define meditation as being the loving, suffering and participating knowledge of something; and contemplation as the reflective awareness of one's own self in this meditation. The meditating person submerges himself in the object of his meditation. He is absorbed in the contemplation of it. He 'forgets himself'. The object is submerged in him. In contemplation he recollects himself once more. He becomes conscious of the changes in himself. He comes back to himself, having gone out of himself and forgotten himself. In meditation we become aware of the object. In the contemplation that is bound up with it we become aware of our awareness. Of course there is no meditation without contemplation and no contemplation without meditation; but in discussing knowledge and how we arrive at it, it is useful to make the distinction.

This has certain consequences for the Christian faith.

(*a*) Christian meditation is not transcendental meditation. It is meditation on an object. It is in its innermost nature *meditatio passionis et mortis Christi* – meditation on Christ's passion and death: the stations of the cross, meditation on the passion, Good Friday mysticism.[5] The history of Christ is recognized as being an open, inclusive history, a history 'for us'. His giving of himself to death 'for us' makes that apparent once and for all. That is why this history of Christ is accessible to the knowledge mediated through meditation – the participatory knowledge, that is to say, which transforms the knower. The observer is drawn into the open history of Christ. He does not apply Christ's history to himself; he applies himself – refers himself – to Christ's history. Then he discovers himself again in that history. He participates in it, finding himself accepted, reconciled, and liberated for God's kingdom. His life-history becomes a part of the life-history of God in Christ.

(*b*) When the person who is meditating on the history of

62

Christ is recalled to himself, he discovers that what he knows of the history of Christ is determined by that history itself. As he finds the 'Christ for us', 'Christ is in him'. Then he comes to know the history of the Christ who was crucified *for* him in the presence of the Spirit of the Christ who is risen *in* him. Just by knowing nothing except Jesus Christ and him crucified (I Cor. 2.2), he can say with Paul, 'It is no longer I who live, but Christ who lives in me' (Gal. 2.20). Just as, according to Paul, 'the fellowship of Christ's sufferings' and 'the power of his resurrection' are experienced simultaneously in faith, so the self-forgetting knowledge of the history of the cross of Christ *extra nos* and the self-knowing perception of the risen Christ *in nobis* belong together as a single whole. The meditative knowledge of Christ *pro nobis* and the contemplative perception of Christ *in nobis* require one another reciprocally.

If we ignore what Albert Schweitzer called 'the mysticism of the apostle Paul' and are aware merely of the 'Christ for us' in word and sacrament, we easily become orthodox in a sterile and institutionalized way. But if we depart from word and sacrament, and so from the open history of 'Christ for us', in order to give ourselves up entirely to the mysticism focused on Christ, we lose sight of Christ by losing sight of his history. We lose ourselves in nothingness. The conflict between the orthodoxy of the 'established' churches in Germany and Pietism, with its freer spirit, was fought out on this pernicious alternative between 'Christ for us' and 'Christ within us'. We can avoid the alternative between salvation as something objective and salvation as something subjective if we discover the open, inclusive history of Christ, and the history of our own lives within that history of Christ. For our own history with Christ's history is called the history of the Holy Spirit and is understood as such. Without the contemplative perception of the Holy Spirit's activity 'in us', the history of Christ 'for us' does not come alive; and the reverse is equally true.

We called contemplation the awareness of our awareness of Christ's history. But because awareness of an objective awareness is not in itself objective, particular wariness is called for. It is an indirect knowing of knowledge and awareness of the self that is given together with the consciousness of the object as such. As long as knowledge is viewed as an *activity* on the part of the knower, this knowing of knowledge is an awareness of subjectivity. But this cannot be maintained, since awareness again presupposes subjectivity, and so on. It is a different matter if knowing can be viewed as the activity of the counterpart, which lays itself open to the act of knowing. Then knowing is a *suffering* of impressions and is based on the knower's active receptivity. Knowledge of knowing that is constituted in *this* way leads to consciousness of our own objectivity. That is the meaning of the wise old saying, 'to know God means to suffer God'. And this we *can* maintain. The changes which the impressions perceived make in the knower can be consciously realized through contemplation.

But this raises a question. What happens to the knower through his knowledge of the history of Christ? What effect does the Holy Spirit have in the fellowship of Christ? The traditional theological answer is: the restoration of man as God's image, the gift to the believer of God's friendship, and ultimately likeness to God in the glory of God. Man becomes the image of Christ, and being the image of Christ he becomes God's likeness. Knowledge of Christ therefore leads to 'the birth of God in the soul'.

It is only possible to stress this subjective side of faith in Christ as emphatically as mysticism does, if contemplation is prepared to investigate this renewal, liberation and perfecting of the believer's soul in God. As far as the activity of the knowing person is concerned, everything is directed towards the object of his cognition. But as far as his receptivity is concerned, everything – even the object of his cognition – is directed towards him himself. The open history of Christ 'for us' is therefore continued in his history 'with us' and 'in us', and in our history 'in him' and 'with him'. The subjective goal of this history is the restoration of the believer as God's image. This is what contemplation considers. This is the process of which it makes us aware. Being the image of God is understood here as man's destiny and his capacity for beholding God. It is only fulfilled in the beatific vision when, with open face, we see God face to face.

The motto Augustine took for mysticism was 'God and the soul'. Enough criticism has been levied against this in modern times (by myself among others) for it now to be legitimate to stress its positive meaning. The correlation of the two words has nothing to do with a Neoplatonic preference for the soul, as compared with the body. What Augustine is concerned with is man's *self*, since he has been created in God's image and in order to become God's image. In other words, 'God and the soul' means 'God and his image on earth'. God is known through his image in his image on earth. This does not necessarily mean forgetfulness of the world or hatred of the body.

William of St Thierry, a friend of Bernard of Clairvaux, makes God say: 'Know thyself, since thou art my image. So shalt thou know me, whose image thou art, and so shalt thou find me in thyself.' And a pseudo-Bernardine text runs: 'In vain doth a man raise the eye of his heart to the knowledge of God if he be not able first to know himself. For first it is required of thee to contemplate what is invisible in thine own spirit, before thou canst be capable of knowing what is invisible in God ... The pre-eminent and chief mirror in which we see God is our own reasonable soul, in so far as it finds itself.' Hugh of St Victor points the same way: 'To ascend to God, that means to enter into the self, and not to enter into self solely, but to go beyond it in one's innermost being in a way that is inexpressible. He therefore who enters with supreme inwardness into himself, who passes through himself in his innermost being and who rises above himself – he in very truth ascends to God.'

The theological goal of the soul's mystical journey to God is to be found in the soul's likeness to God and in our recognition that the saving purpose of the history of Christ was to restore man as God's image, and to consummate that likeness by making human beings like God. The world is God's creation, but not his image. Only the human person was destined to be God's image. God is more visible in his image than in his works. The knowledge of the objective world is knowledge mediated through the senses, and is hence always partly deceptive. But the soul's knowledge of itself is a knowledge which is not mediated through the senses, so it is more assured. Love for God's creation is love for his works. Love for human beings is love of his image. Direct love of God's image is love of the self. That is why, according to Bernard of Clairvaux, love of our neighbour begins with love of ourselves: love thy neighbour as thyself, not vice versa. Love of the self as love of God's image in oneself is a step towards the love of God, and part of it. Finally, the idea that God's image in human beings is a mirror can lead to Meister Eckhart's radical and problematical identification of knowledge of the self with knowledge of God: God knows himself in his image. The person who recognizes that he is himself this image, recognizes God in himself and himself in God, and God recognizes himself in him. His knowledge of God in himself is God's knowledge of himself in him. God's knowledge of himself and man's knowledge of himself are one: 'The eye wherein I see God is the same eye wherein God sees me; my eye and God's eye are one eye, one vision, one knowing, one love.'[6]

This brings us to the step which leads from contemplation

to the *unio mystica*, mystical union. We are led to this step through the contemplation of the meditation on the history of Christ. As we become conscious of ourselves in this history, the image of God for which we are created is restored. As this happens we know ourselves in God and 'God in us', mediated through ourselves in our character as God's image. Can there actually be a further step to God beyond this? Can we acquire more than indirect knowledge of God? 'The man who looks on God must die,' says the Old Testament. So the indirect knowledge of God in and through his image on earth is not simply a hindrance; it is also a protection for men and women. Consequently knowledge of Christ's divinity through his manhood is not simply a veiling of God; it is also intended as a gracious sparing of man. God's hiddenness in his revelation is grace, not affliction. God's absence in his presence is liberation, not estrangement. And yet the passion of the person who seeks God and fulfilment in God thrusts forward beyond the mediations into what is direct and unmediated.

Let me sum up what I have tried to say in a little story. I have changed the names so that you in my audience can put yourself into the story.

'A long time ago a young man was living here in Kalamazoo. He was very poor, had no work, and lived in a dilapidated little hut on the edge of the town. One night he had a dream. He saw a huge treasure, buried under a bridge in a strange city, which he did not recognize. The name of the city was Prague. When he woke up, he seized his spade and set out. He made his way right across America to the east coast, took a ship to Europe, and wandered through many European countries until he finally came to Prague. There he found the bridge he had dreamed about. He waited until it was dark, and then he began to dig. For seven whole nights he dug and dug, and found – nothing at all. On the seventh night he suddenly saw another boy standing on the bridge. The boy watched him digging and asked him what he was doing. When the young man told him about the dream he had had in his hut in America, the boy on the bridge laughed, and said: "Last night I had a very similar dream. I saw a treasure buried under the bed in a dilapidated little hut. The hut was on the edge of a little town with a funny name: Kalamazoo. But all the same, I'm not mad enough to go there." But the young man understood the message. He picked up his spade, made his way through the countries of Europe until he reached a port, took a ship and crossed the Atlantic. When he got to America he walked and walked through the forests until at last he arrived in Kalamazoo. He found his dilapidated little hut again, pushed aside the bed, began to dig – and found the treasure he had dreamed about. And so he became a rich man.'


EXPERIENCE OF GOD IN THE WORLD


### 3 Contemplation and Mystical Union

We are now considering mysticism in the narrower sense of the *unio mystica*, mystical union: the moment of fulfilment, the ecstasy of union, the submerging of the soul in what the mystics describe as 'the infinite ocean of the Godhead'. This moment is dark, unknowable and inexpressible. Because it can only be experienced with the whole soul or not at all, no one can be present to observe it or to be sensible of it.

So because we cannot talk about it we must be silent. But in order through this silence to describe the mystic stillness (*silentium mysticum*) in the unveiled presence of God, we are bound to speak. We are bound to speak in order to abolish speech. The mediations through which the soul arrived at communion with God have to be abolished, so that the soul does not linger at them, but uses them for what they are: the rungs of a ladder, the hand-rails on a path, the stages of a journey. All the mystics have talked about the abolition of the mediations, for man's love for God is enticed and drawn by God's love for man. Just as God descended to man in his love, so man's love ascends to God, on the paths struck out by God himself, in creation, incarnation and the sending of the Spirit.

This can be understood to take place so simply that, from the gifts of grace for which it prays and for which it gives thanks, faith finds and grasps the *gracious hand* of God, from which these gifts come. From this gracious hand of God, faith moves to the *open heart* of God; so that it finally loves God no longer for his gifts of grace, or for his gracious hand, or even for the loving indulgence with which he bestows these things; it loves him simply for his own sake. On this ladder love is withdrawn from the objects of love in creation and directed towards God himself. It is diverted even from the visible image of God, and directed to God in his own archetypal being. The mystics face man with the alternative: what do you love? God or the world? But they do so, not in the sense of a gnostic contempt of the world, but in the sense of love's detachment from secondary objects. In order to free all created beings and man himself from man's infinite, and therefore destructive, love of God, they demand the 'work of grief', which means stripping bare, estrangement, poverty, the abandonment of everything, and finally even the self-annihilation of the soul itself. Man's love for God is withdrawn from the world and the self. This means the end of the service of idols, which idolatrous love of the world and the self pursues with such neurotic compulsion. The strain put on the world and the self is ended through the love of God. Creation and the self become free for what they are when God is loved and enjoyed in eternity for his own sake.

Meister Eckhart described this abolition of the mediations

of God with particular logical stringency in his treatise 'On Detachment'. The love which has been withdrawn from *creation* through God (who is love's true fulfilment) is directed first of all towards the *Creator*. But God continues to withdraw it from the Creator of all things, guiding it towards *God himself*. It leaves the Trinity behind and enters into the womb of the divine nature. It finally leaves 'God for us' and turns wholly towards 'God in himself', in order to enter into God's separation and detachment from the world and, through its own separation and detachment, to correspond to God's detachment. Eckhart heightens this detachment in almost exaggerated form:

When God created the heaven and the earth, he might not have been making anything at all for all it affected his detachment. . . . When the Son in his Godhead was pleased to be made man, and . . . suffered martyrdom, God's motionless detachment was no more disturbed than if he had never been made man.

Eckhart describes the mystery in paradoxical and apophatic terms: 'Detachment is altogether naught'; and when the soul in its detachment comes to resemble the detachment of God, then it is 'ignorant with knowing, loveless with loving, dark with enlightenment'.[7]

In his sermon 'Qui audit me' he reduces the detachment of love-stripped-bare to the well-known formula: 'Let God go, for God's sake.'[8] We can call this 'mystical atheism'. But it is atheism in God, 'for God's sake'.

Meister Eckhart expressed this abolition of all the mediations in the progress of the soul's journey home to God in his sermon 'Beati pauperes spiritu':

Granting a man is bare of everything, of creatures, of himself, of God, yet if it is still in him to provide God with the room to work in . . .

– and then he goes on to abolish even this 'room' too.

As we should say, he was a man too poor to have or be a place for God to work in. To preserve place is to preserve distinction. . . . Poverty of spirit means freedom from God and all his works, so that if God chooses to travail in the soul, he must be his own workshop, as he likes to be. . . . then God is his own patient and he is his own operating room, since God is in himself the operation.[9]

The breaking of the shell, so as to reach the kernel; the abolition of the mediations, so as to arrive at the goal; and the stage by stage withdrawal of created things, revelations and divine condescensions, so that God may be loved in himself; the abolition of God for God's sake – these are the ultimate possibilities of the mystical journey which are expressible at all.

Let us sum up the different steps. Action led us to meditation. Meditation on the history of Christ for us led us to contemplation of the presence of his Spirit in us, and to the restoration of ourselves as God's image. The road from contemplation to the mystical moment leads (as Eckhart makes plain) to the abolition of man's likeness to God for God's sake, and ultimately to the abolition of God for God's sake. Then the soul has found its way home; then love has found bliss; then passion ends in infinite enjoyment; then like is with like. But is this really the goal of union with Christ? I believe not. I believe we must look in a completely different direction and take an entirely different path.

### 4  Mysticism and Discipleship

The mystical way is always described as the soul's journey into loneliness, into silence and remoteness, into the throwing off, stripping away and abandonment of all earthly and physical things, into the inner self-emptying and letting go of all spiritual things, and finally into 'the dark night of the soul'. If we ask about the actual experience of this journey and its

*Sitz im Leben* – its background in real life – the answer we get is not religious at all; it is political. We meet, not the monk, but the martyr. 'Blessed are those who are persecuted for righteousness' sake, for theirs is the kingdom of heaven' (Matt. 5.10).

In prison, the person who is persecuted for righteousness' sake is stripped of everything he loves. He is cut off from all human relationships. Celibacy is forced on him. Under torture, his nakedness is laid bare and he is subjected to physical mortifications. He loses his name and becomes a number. His spiritual identity is destroyed by drugs. In the silent cell he falls into the dark night of the soul.[10] If he is executed, he dies 'outside the camp' (Heb. 13.13) 'with Christ' and is buried with him 'in his death'. The way of mystical experience is really the way of discipleship and resistance against the oppression of men and women.

The place of mystical experience is in very truth the cell – the prison cell. The 'witness to the truth of Christ' is despised, scoffed at, persecuted, dishonoured and rejected. In his own fate he experiences the fate of Christ. His fate conforms to Christ's fate. This is what the mystics called *conformitas crucis*, the conformity of the cross. That is why he also experiences the presence of the risen Christ in the fellowship of Christ's sufferings, and the deeper the fellowship in suffering is, the surer he becomes of Christ's presence. Eckhart's remark that suffering is the shortest way to the birth of God in the soul applies, not to any imagined suffering, but to the very real sufferings endured by 'the witness to the truth'. God in the cell, God in the interrogation, God in the torture, God in the body's agony, God in that spiritual derangement which is the dark night of the soul – all this is the mystic experience of the martyr. It is not going too far to say that prison is the place where the deepest experience of Christian liberty is to be found. In prison the spiritual presence of Christ is felt. In prison the soul finds the *unio mystica.* This is what the 'cloud of witnesses' in Korea, South Africa, Latin America and other countries tells us. The Catholic poet and martyr Kim Chi Ha speaks for many others. He was condemned to death for his part in a Christian Koinonia revolution in South Korea. The death penalty was later commuted to life imprisonment. In *Leidensweg 1974*, written while he was in prison, he says:

In this cell every second was death. The confrontation with death. The struggle with death. Was one to get the better of oneself in this confrontation and achieve the inner liberty of the warrior. or should one surrender in ignominy and defeat?

The way of suffering in the mystery of the cross means overcoming death by deciding for death. That was our task.

Church history too points back from the mystical piety of the cloister to the experience of the martyrs in their prison cells. The spiritual discipleship of Christ in the soul tries to correspond to discipleship in actual human, political contexts. Devotion to the stations of the cross is an echo of the very real sufferings of the martyrs. It is true that on the way from martyrdom to mysticism fellowship with Christ is raised to another level: following him becomes imitation of him, the suffering of humiliation becomes the virtue of humility, external persecution becomes inner temptation, and murder and execution become 'spiritual death'.

Yet through the mysticism that is centred on Christ the remembrance of Christ's sufferings and the sufferings of the martyrs is kept alive. This means a firmly held hope for the future of Christ in history. As long as we do not think that dying with Christ spiritually is a substitute for dying with him in reality, mysticism does not mean estrangement from action; it is a preparation for public, political discipleship. As long as we do not interpret the dark night of the soul metaphysically, but see it in quite concrete terms as the experience of Golgotha, that dark night points beyond itself to the death of the witness himself. Whereas medieval and baroque mysticism saw their goal as being the purification of the soul, from the time of John of the Cross onwards the idea of participation in Christ's passion increasingly gained ground. In Theresa of Lisieux it was a mystical and physically suffered *compassio Christi*. Her experience of dying in the absence of God links the mysticism centred on Christ with martyrdom and with everyday life. Believers are not simply the passive recipients of the fruits of Christ's passion. They are counted worthy to suffer with Christ, so that like him they may become fruitful for the kingdom of God, as John 12.24f. promises of the grain of corn that falls into the ground and dies.

Mysticism and discipleship belong together and are of vital importance for the church which calls itself by the name of Christ. The apostles were also martyrs. The church was called to life out of their message and their suffering. Paul's catalogues of suffering (Rom. 8; I Cor. 4; II Cor. 6, 11 and 12) are not related because they were stories about Paul personally. They have a power that testifies to the gospel. They are an expression of the apostolic mediation between Christ's passion and the apocalyptic sufferings of the world. Pauline eschatology is *theologia crucis* because his theology of the cross is the profoundest expression of hope for Christ's coming. The apostolic sufferings are not sufferings *for* Christ, in the sense that a soldier dies for his country. They are sufferings *with* Christ, in which the apocalyptic sufferings of the world are accepted by Christ's people and are overcome through the power of his resurrection. Suffering leads Christ's witness deeper and deeper into fellowship with him. Because his own suffering brings this about, he expresses the eschatological hope on behalf of the whole creation, in its fears and anxieties. The person who accepts *his own* suffering, and does not run away from it, shows the power of hope. So Erik Peterson was right when he wrote: 'The apostolic church, which is founded on the apostles who became martyrs, is always at the same time the suffering church, the church of the martyrs.'

As an established religion, and in its bourgeois form, Christianity has become estranged from this truth.

Passion mysticism cannot be a substitute for this. It must be the echo and preparation of Christ's church, which lives in its martyrs.

What does this mean for us?

It is useful to prepare for the prison cell in the monastery cell. Dietrich Bonhoeffer did this in the monastery at Ettal, before he was arrested and put in prison in Tegel. It is useful to learn to be alone and to be silent before we are condemned to these things. It is liberating to sink into the wounds of the risen Christ in meditation, so as to experience our own torments as his fate. It is redemptive to find God in the depths of our own souls before we are cut off from the outside world through some act of violence. The person who has died in Christ before he dies, though he die, yet shall he live.

Finally, like the particular paths of the mystic and the martyr, everyday life in the world also has its secret mysticism and its quiet martyrdom. The soul does not only die with Christ and become 'cruciform' by means of spiritual exercises and in public martyrdom. It already takes the form of the cross in the pains of life and the sufferings of love. The history of the suffering, forsaken and crucified Christ is so open that the suffering, forsakenness and anxieties of every loving man or woman find a place in it and are accepted. If they find a place in it and are accepted, it is not in order to give them permanence, but in order to transform and heal them. Suffering with Christ includes even the uncomprehending pain of a child and the inconsolable suffering of helpless parents. It includes the frustrations and the public oppression of the weak and the unimportant. It even includes the apocalyptic suffering that has not yet been

experienced. Because it has taken in the whole divine judgment, there is nothing which is alien to it, and nothing,
either, which would have to alienate us from Christ. That is
why the experience of the risen 'Christ in us' is not merely
to be found in the heights of spiritual contemplation or in
the depths of the martyr's death, but even in the little experiences of suffering that is sustained and transformed. Anyone
who loves dies many deaths. The life that is life with Christ
consoles us when we have to go on living and gives us hope
for the resurrection of love. It strengthens the power to resist
of the weak and unimportant, when they are disheartened
by the strong. It gives creative energy where no possibilities
seem open to us any more. The person who is alive experiences many resurrections. The mystics and the martyrs are
exceptions; but there is also an everyday *meditatio crucis in
passione mundi* which many people practise without realiz-
ing it.

There is the simple experience of resurrection wherever
there are experiences of love. We are in God and God is in
us wherever we are wholly and individually present. Probably
this mysticism of everyday life is the deepest mysticism of all.
The acceptance of the lowliness of one's own life is the true
humility. Simple existence is life in God. For in what Ernst
Bloch called the 'darkness of the lived moment', the beginning and the end are both present. Here time is eternity and
eternity is time. In the existence that is unforeseen and unex-
pected, everything is transformed 'in a moment' 'at the last
trumpet' (I Cor. 15.52). The mystical *kairos* is the divine
secret of life. To find it is so easy and therefore so difficult.
The key to the secret is childlikeness and wonder, or – in the
word of an earlier piety – simplicity.

## 5 The Vision of the World in God

Mysticism has continually been reproached with contempt for the world and hatred of the body. And it is easy enough to bring evidence to prove the existence of ideas drawn from Neoplatonic idealism and Gnostic dualism in the writings of the mystical theologians. So it is all the more surprising to find in many of them a pantheistic vision of the world in God, and God in the world. 'All is one and one is all in God' says the *Theologia Germanica*; and for the poet monk and Nicaraguan revolutionary Ernesto Cardenal the whole of nature is simply 'palpable, materialized divine love', 'the reflection of his beauty', and 'full of love letters to us'.

The mystical theologians undoubtedly recognize the Old Testament doctrine of creation in the form in which it was maintained in the dogmatic teachings of the church. But for their own vision of *the world from God* they prefer the expressions 'pouring' and 'flowing', 'source' and 'fountain', 'sun' and 'shining'. And for their vision of *the world in God* they use expressions such as 'homecoming', 'entering in', 'sinking' and 'dissolving'. Looked at as part of the history of thought, this is the Neoplatonic language of the emanation of all things from the All-One, and the remanation in the All-One. But interpreted theologically it is the language of pneumatology. The Holy Spirit is 'poured out' on all flesh (Joel 2.28ff.; Acts 2.16ff.) and into our hearts (Rom. 5.5) in a way that is different from creation and the 'works' of God in history. We are 'born again' from the Spirit (John 3.3), not created by it. The gifts of the Spirit are not created *ex nihilo*, out of nothing. They derive from the Holy Spirit itself. They are divine energies. The life-giving Spirit 'fills' creation with eternal life by 'descending' on all and 'dwelling' in them. A different divine presence is revealed in the history of the Holy Spirit from the presence revealed in creation in the beginning. Men and women in their physical nature (I Cor.

6.13–20), and then the new heaven and the new earth, become the temple in which God himself dwells. This is the eternal sabbath; the rest of God and rest in God.

That is why the history of the Spirit is directed towards that consummation which Paul describes in a pantheistic-sounding phrase: 'that God may be all in all' (I Cor. 15.28 AV). This history of the Spirit which will be poured out on all flesh, and this new world which is glorified in God, is what the mystical theologians mean with their doctrine of creation and redemption, with its Neoplatonic overtones. 'He that possesses God thus', said Meister Eckhart, 'that is to say, in his very being, that man takes God in his divinity, and to that man God shines in all things; for all things taste to him of God, and God's image is visible to him in all things.'[11]

This conceals a new and specifically Christian vision of reality, which is stamped by belief in the incarnation of the Son and the experience of the indwelling of the divine Spirit. The church's reiteration of the doctrine of creation as we find it in the Yahwist and the Priestly Writing cannot be regarded as a creative achievement on the part of Christian theology. This doctrine of creation can be either Christian or non-Christian. It suggests a gap between Creator and created being (as the image of the Creator) which is not in accordance with the intimate Christian experience of God. If it is true that the Israelite doctrine of the creation reflects Israel's experience of the exodus, then surely the Christian doctrine of creation ought to reflect Christianity's experience of Christ and the Spirit? Theologically, mystical 'pantheism' is certainly not a particularly successful step in this direction, but it *is* at least a step. Gregory Palamas' teachings about the energies of the Holy Spirit takes us further here: 'The world is overflowing with divine power, which works in it and illuminates it.'

Let us return to the reason for this pantheistic vision of

the world in God. In Christ's death on the cross, God took evil, sin and rejection on himself, transforming it into goodness, grace and election in the sacrifice of his infinite love. All evil, all sin, suffering and damnation is 'in God'. They have been endured by him, abolished in him, transformed by him. These are 'the benefits of his passion' for us. His suffering is what Paul of the Cross called 'the wonder of wonders of divine love'. Nothing can be excluded from it. Everything that lives therefore lives from the almighty power of his suffering love, and out of the inexhaustibility of his self-giving love. There is no longer any Nothingness to threaten creation in its existence. For Nothingness has been destroyed in God. Immortal being has been manifested. Because of the cross of Christ, creation already lives from God and is transformed in God.

Without the cross of Christ this vision of God in the world would be pure optimistic illusion. The suffering of one, single child would prove it to be so. Without the recognition of the suffering of God's inexhaustible love no 'pantheism' can endure in this world of death. It would soon become pannihilism.

It is the knowledge of the crucified God which gives this vision of the world in God foundation and permanence. The person who believes that God is to be found in the Godforsakenness of the crucified Jesus believes that he sees God everywhere, in all things; just as after we have experienced what death is like, we experience life more intensely every moment, because every moment seems unique.

This vision of God's world is alive in the experience of the persecuted and the martyrs who feel God's presence in prison. It is alive in the mystics, who find God's presence in the dark night of the soul. It shines in the devotion of the simple, to whom God is present in the darkness of the lived moment. 'In him we live and move and have our being' (Acts

18.28), for 'from him and through him and to him are all things' (Rom. 11.36).

Let me illustrate what I should like to say with another story, which I found in Martin Buber.

We are told that once upon a time a man filled with a passion for God left the realm of created things and entered into the great emptiness. He wandered about there until he found himself before the gate to the great Mystery. He knocked. Someone within called out: 'What do you want?' 'I have proclaimed thy praise to the ears of mortal men and women', said the man, 'but they were deaf to it. So now I come to thee, so that thou thyself mayest hear me and answer.' 'Turn back', said the voice. 'There is no one to listen to you here. I have sunk my hearing in the deafness of mortal men and women.'

This is the Christian experience of God too. Suppose we saw the heavens open, like Jacob in his dream. Suppose there were a ladder up to heaven, and that we were able to climb the ladder into heaven itself, so that we were at last able to see God face to face. Whom should we find there? We should find the babe lying in the manger. We should find ourselves standing before the Man on the cross. *Ecce Deus* – there is God. And whoever wants to find him must look for him in the fellowship of Jesus Christ. He will find God at the foot of the cross on Golgotha.

# Notes

### Why am I a Christian?

1. Franz Rosenzweig, *Der Stern der Erlösung*, Heidelberg 1954³, Book III, p. 192.
2. Dietrich Bonhoeffer, letter to E. Bethge, 16 July 1944, ET in *Letters and Papers from Prison*, enlarged edition, SCM Press and Macmillan, New York 1971, p. 361.

### Anxiety

1. S. Kierkegaard, *The Concept of Dread*, ET Princeton University Press and OUP 1944, p. 139 (altered).
2. E. Bloch, *Das Prinzip Hoffnung*, Frankfurt 1959, Vol. I, p. 1.
3. Kierkegaard and Bloch both maintained the same principle: that potentiality is higher than reality. Anxiety and hope are both ways of experiencing the possible. But a closer comparison of the concept of possibility in Kierkegaard and Bloch would discover differences. Kierkegaard writes (op. cit., pp. 139f.): 'He who is educated by dread is educated by possibility, and only the man who is educated by possibility is educated in accordance with his infinity. Possibility is therefore the heaviest of all categories.'
Bloch writes (op. cit., p. 5): 'Expectation, hope, intention towards still unrealized potentiality: all this is not merely a fundamental characteristic of the human consciousness but, specifically corrected and understood, is a fundamental mood within objective reality as a whole.' Bloch is interested in 'the realization of potentiality' in the sense of active hope, not, like Kierkegaard, in the sense of dread of its becoming possible.
4. Kierkegaard, op. cit., p. 139: 'Dread is the possibility of freedom.' Bloch, op. cit., pp. 1392f.
5. Robert Browning, *Christmas Eve*, V, lines 23–25.
6. On the theology of the following passage cf. J. Moltmann, *The Crucified God*, ET SCM Press and Harper & Row 1974.
7. The familiar English translation, however, does not bring out the full force of the German. What Paul Gerhardt actually writes is: 'snatch me

out of my *fears* through thy *fear* and suffering' (Dann reiss mich aus den Ängsten/kraft deiner Angst und Pein') [Translator].

8. Cf. also D. S. Merezhkovsky's interpretation in *Tod und Auferstehung*, Leipzig 1935, pp. 176ff.

9. Quoted in E. Vogelsang, *Der angefochtene Christus bei Luther*, Berlin and Leipzig 1932, pp. 44f.

10. Ibid., pp. 22ff., 40ff.

11. O. Michel, *Der Brief an die Hebräer*, Göttingen 1949[8], p. 74: 'The reading χωρὶς Θεοῦ [without God] is to be preferred, textually. God leads Christ into suffering (2.10), but at the same time increases this suffering through the assailment of being forsaken by God (Mark 15.34).'

12. Paul Gerhardt:

| Paul Gerhardt: | Trans J. Kelly: |
|---|---|
| Ich hang und bleib auch hangen | Now I will cling for ever |
| an Christus als ein Glied. | To Christ, my Saviour true; |
| Wo mein Haupt durch ist gangen, | My Lord will leave me never, |
| da nimmt es mich auch mit: | Whate'er he passes through. |
| Er reisset durch den Tod, | He rends death's iron chain; |
| durch Welt, durch Sünd, durch Not, | He breaks through sin and pain, |
| er reisset durch die Höll: | He shatters hell's grim thrall |
| ich bin stets sein Gesell. | I follow him through all. |

13. But again (cf. n.7) the German counterpart to Watts stresses the believer's gratitude for Christ's *fear*:

'für dein Angst und tiefe Pein
will ich ewig dankbar sein.'

Sensitivity to this element of Christ's passion seems to be particularly present among the German hymn-writers [Translator].

14. M. de Unamuno, *The Tragic Sense of Life in Men and Nations*, ET, Selected Works, Vol. 4, Routledge & Kegan Paul and Princeton University Press 1972, p. 223. Cf. also R. Garcia Mateo, *Dialektik als Polemik. Welt, Bewusstsein, Gott bei Miguel de Unamuno*, Frankfurt 1978, esp. pp. 148ff., 'The Suffering God'. Mateo writes: 'These remarks of Unamuno today agree, broadly speaking, with Moltmann's theology of the cross' (p. 157). I can only partially agree, since I am unable to believe that Christ's crucifixion was either a human tragedy or a divine one.

15. Unamuno, op. cit., p. 227.

16. N. Berdyaev, *The Meaning of History*, ET Geoffrey Bles and Scribner's 1936, pp. 45, 48, 55 (altered). Cf. also his *Spirit and Reality*, ET Bles and Scribner's 1939, pp. 106f.: 'It was not only the most just of men who was thus crucified, but also the Son of God. Unjust suffering was divine suffering. And unjust divine suffering proved to be an expiation of all human suffering. . . . Suffering is . . . a mystery and a secret. Suffering is a mystery because it can also become expiation.'

17. On the theology behind this view cf. J. Moltmann, 'Die trinitarische Geschichte Gottes', *EvTh* 35, 1975, pp. 208–23.

## The Theology of Mystical Experience

1. M. Luther, *Randbemerkungen zu Tauler* (1516), Clemen, V, p. 306: 'Unde totus iste sermo procedit ex theologia mystica, quae est sapientia experimentalis et non doctrinalis.'
2. Cf. E. Cardenal, *Das Buch der Liebe*, with preface by Thomas Merton, Siebensterntaschenbuch, 1976⁴, p. 168.
3. K. Marx, *Die Frühschriften*, ed. S. Landshut, Stuttgart 1953, p. 275.
4. Cf. Thomas Merton, *Contemplation in a World of Action*, Allen & Unwin 1971, Image Books, New York 1973; cf. also *The Cloud of Unknowing* and *The Epistle of Privy Counsel*.
5. On the Protestant side, an example is the devotion to the cross we find in Count Zinzendorf, the founder of the Herrnhut (Moravian) brethren. A Roman Catholic parallel is the devotion to the passion we find in St Paul of the Cross, the founder of the Passionist order.
6. *Meister Eckhart*, ET by C. de B. Evans, Vol. I, London 1924, p. 240.
7. Ibid., I, pp. 340–8; quotations from pp. 343, 342, and 346. (Cf. also Meister Eckhart, *Selected Treatises and Sermons*, trans. J. M. Clark and J. V. Skinner, Fontana Books 1963, pp. 156–67.)
8. Sermon 96, ibid., I, p. 239.
9. Ibid., I, p. 220. The idea of the abolition of the mediations of God through man's love for God brings Christian mysticism surprisingly close to Zen. Cf. T. Merton, *Zen and the Birds of Appetite*, New Directions, New York 1968; *Mystics and Zen Masters*, Dell, New York 1969.
10. John of the Cross composed his great poem 'The Dark Night of the Soul' in a prison cell in the Carmelite monastery in Toledo. Cf. his *Complete Works*, trans. E. Allison Peers, new edition, Burns, Oates & Washbourne 1953, Vol. I, pp. 325–7, 421–7; W. Herbstrith, *Therese von Lisieux. Anfechtung und Solidarität*, Frankfurt 1974². H. Urs von Balthasar describes this 'dark night' quite soberly: 'That the way of contemplation, honourably and unswervingly followed, usually passes into darkness: into a state in which nothing is seen any longer, a state which has been prayed for and for which renunciations have been made, a state of no longer knowing whether God still listens, still wants the sacrifice, still receives it . . .' (*Who is a Christian?*, ET Burns & Oates 1968, p. 78).
11. Meister Eckhart, *Deutsche Predigten und Schriften*, ed. and trans. H. Quint, Munich 1977⁴, p. 60.